SOUTHEAST ASIA
AND THE WORLD TODAY

CLAUDE A. BUSS

Professor of History
Stanford University

AN ANVIL ORIGINAL

under the general editorship of

LOUIS L. SNYDER

D. VAN NOSTRAND COMPANY, INC.

PRINCETON, NEW JERSEY

TORONTO   LONDON

NEW YORK

Dedicated to three lively Locsin boys in Manila and to three lovely grandchildren in Denver. May the world for them be equally free from heartaches and equally brimming with opportunity and with happiness.

D. VAN NOSTRAND COMPANY, INC.

120 Alexander St., Princeton, New Jersey (*Principal office*)
257 Fourth Avenue, New York 10, New York
25 Hollinger Rd., Toronto 16, Canada
358, Kensington High Street, London, W.14, England

REFACE — *53774*

Southeast Asians are part of our world; we must dis-
over theirs. From Canton to Calcutta has been an Amer-
an no-man's land, as unknown as Africa. For centuries
e British concerned themselves with India, Burma, and
lalaya; the French with Indochina; and the Dutch with
e Indies—but the first real sparks of American interest
the region were generated by the Spanish-American
ar. At that time President McKinley confessed that he
uld not have told within a thousand miles where the
ilippines were located.

Interest in Southeast Asia grew with the automobile
dustry and its insatiable demand for tires. Canning com-
nies needed Southeast Asian tin. American dollars paid
r much of the prewar wealth of the Indies—but too
ten the dollars continued in transit to European in-
stors or imperial governments without bringing ade-
ate development or reasonable happiness to neglected
oples of Southeast Asia.

It is not that the masses were entirely neglected or
at the record of imperialism was all bad. Each power—
reat Britain, France, the Netherlands, Portugal, and
ain—considered primarily its own interests, and only
condarily the welfare of its distant subjects. The Euro-
ans prided themselves on their record; the Asians be-
me more impatient for a greater share of the profits
d for more political rights. Asians resented the differ-
ce between their poverty and European wealth, be-
een western democracy at home and imperialism over-
as.

Dreams of economic prosperity and social justice fired
sian souls. Cautious agitation for small benefits grew
to great campaigns for self-government and independ-
ce. Adjustments in the policies of mother countries were
hurried and inadequate. Martyrs and heroes were born
cause of firing squads, scaffolds, islands of exile, and
ison cells—the traditional instruments for the preserva-
n of colonial law and order. Asians found inspiration

in Japan's defeat of Russia at the turn of the century an
took new hope in President Wilson's electric message c
self-determination. Pleas for peaceful change becam
shouts for revolution. World War II unexpectedly relieve
the white man of his burden. Southeast Asians assume
their own responsibilities.

The author traveled extensively in Southeast Asia be
fore World War II. He was in Manila as Executive Assis
ant to the United States High Commissioner to the Philip
pines when Japan attacked at Pearl Harbor. In 1957 h
lectured as a Fulbright exchange professor at the Univer
sity of the Philippines, and during that time he visite
every country in Southeast Asia except the Democrati
Republic of Vietnam. He and his travel companions wis
to express their special thanks to friends and teacher
correspondents, and unnamed officials who with their ur
failing courtesy and warm hospitality made it such a de
light to gather these materials and assemble this inform;
tion.

Stanford University,   C.A.B.
January, 1958

´ABLE OF CONTENTS

PART 1. SOUTHEAST ASIA

PART II. READINGS

Part I

SOUTHEAST ASIA
AND THE WORLD TODAY

	Sq Mi	Population
Indonesia	735,865	81,000,000
Thailand	200,148	22,800,000
Philippines	115,600	22,000,000
Burma	261,789	19,242,000
North Vietnam	60,000	14,000,000
South Vietnam	65,000	12,000,000
Malaya	52,528	6,058,000
Cambodia	66,800	4,500,000
Laos	89,166	2,500,000
Singapore	220	1,212,000

— 1 —

SOUTHEAST ASIA IN TODAY'S WORLD

The Lands. Southeast Asia is an ageless region where the sense of history is new; where neighbors are scarcely aware of their common experience and mutual interests; where each country is inflamed by an intense—almost anachronistic—spirit of nationalism.

Southeast Asia consists of nine independent states and three colonies. Of the nine, seven are located on the mainland: Thailand (Siam), Burma, Malaya, and the four component parts of former Indochina: the Democratic Republic of Vietnam (DRV or North Vietnam), the Republic of Vietnam (South Vietnam or simply Vietnam), Cambodia, and Laos. The other two are the archipelagoes of Indonesia and the Philippines. The three colonies are Portuguese Timor and the two remaining British colonies of Singapore and British Borneo.

These tropical lands lie in the transition zone between Asia and Australia, and they control the passages between the Indian Ocean and the Pacific Ocean. The continental countries are separated from the rest of Asia by magnificent mountain barriers, and their internal communications are often difficult because of jungles, malarial swamps, or rugged peaks. Where lands divide, the seas unite. Every type of ship—from the Arab sails and the Chinese junks to modern luxury liners—ply from port to port. Airplanes mock the barriers of geography, joining inland villages and island cities with speed and grace known only to the sky.

The strategic value of the lands of Southeast Asia

must be adjudged in terms of the air. The loss of one country to an invading army or an external system does not mean the immediate loss of its neighbor by land; the advantages assigned to island republics in terms of naval power or naval conflict must be reassessed in the realistic light of all the new methods of warfare and weapons known to be available. The strategic value of the position of Southeast Asia is not to be measured in terms of the limited experience of the past, but of the horrible potential of the future.

Each nation is plagued with some problem of political unity. Indonesia's major islands outside of Java and Madura—Sumatra, Kalimantan (Borneo), Sulawesi (Celebes), Malukus (Moluccas or Spice Islands), and Nusa Tenggara (Lesser Sunda Islands comprising Bali, Lombok, Timor, Flores, Savu, etc.,)—are insistent upon greater autonomy. All Indonesia regards West Irian (New Guinea) as rightfully of its own territory. Thailand cannot forget its past influence with Laos, Cambodia, north Malaya, and the Shan states. The Union of Burma is more perfect in name than in fact because of the claims of minority groups including Shans and Karens. The Federation of Malaya must work out a mutually satisfactory arrangement with Singapore; neither half of Vietnam shall cease to bubble and boil politically until the dividing line at the seventeenth parallel is somehow erased.

The People. More people live in Southeast Asia than live in the United States. Most are of coffee-hued Indonesian stock which originated somewhere in southwest China. In some areas they are jammed together as in Java, the Luzon plain, and the deltas of the great rivers like the Red, the Mekong, the Chao Phya, and the Irrawaddy. In other places, population pressure is unknown, as in the Outer Islands of Indonesia, much of Thailand and Burma, and in Mindanao, the large southern islands of the Philippines.

The people of Southeast Asia seem to have some common characteristics—size, color, ethnic origin, food, housing, social structure, and adjustment to climate—but two thousand years of movement and mixture have produced infinite varieties and diversities. Pure races or strains are difficult to isolate. They speak with a thousand tongues. The languages of Indonesia, Malaya, and the Philippines are countless varieties of a common group, and they differ completely from the Austro-Asian and Tibeto-Chinese tongues which are spoken in Thailand and Burma. Some governments are working hard at the creation of a national language, but English is increasingly the *lingua franca* for commerce, higher education, and international communication throughout Southeast Asia.

Southeast Asia has been called the crossroads of religion. Indonesia and Malaya are lands of Mohammedanism: of mosques and minarets; of the Koran, the fez, and frequent calls to prayer. Indonesians vary in interpretations of their religion. They are as interested in a government and social programs as in dogma; they have little regard for fanatical traditions of holy war and hatred of the infidel.

Thailand, Burma, Cambodia, and Laos are classic homes of Buddhism: of pagodas, monasteries, and temples; of yellow-robed monks, priests, and contemplative statues of Lord Buddha. The Philippines are 95 per cent Christian—80 per cent Catholic. Sunday is both holy day and holiday for thousands; these pray and play on that day. They crowd the churches, athletic fields, and movie houses in search for relief from the monotony of the workaday world. In today's world of religious tolerance, Southeast Asia has much to teach as well as to learn. Many of its political arguments and tensions spring from religious divergences.

The Indians and Chinese live side by side with—yet quite apart from—native societies. They intermarry with their own people and preserve their own customs and languages. They are quietly loyal to their own religious convictions, and they perform their own time-honored ceremonials in connection with births, marriages, and funerals. They prosper because of their own ability and the local government's protection of their status and rights. They do not assimilate easily, and they retain at least a degree of ethnic and political pride in the country of their origin.

Psychology. Southeast Asians hate western imperialism and any evidence of racism in the west with a passion. They smoulder over the memory of the exploitation they feel they suffered as colonials. They think they were neglected or abused; treated as pawns in the western struggle for power, prestige, and profit. In a world where education was the open sesame to jobs and opportunities, they point out that in the school year of 1937, for example, the one university in Indochina had but 631 students. In the following semester in all Indonesia there were only 1,100 university students, and most of those were Europeans, Chinese, or Arabs.

Their hopes—which had been stifled during the years of unequal competition against the machines, the wealth, the institutions, and the might of the west—came to life in World War II. The prestige of the white man evaporated. The folly of the west was the opportunity of the east. The rallying cry became independence, no matter the cost, the objections, or the degree of unpreparedness. Independence was the road to Utopia, and the future could take care of its own dilemmas. The leaders—the educated bourgeois elite often abetted by Communists— fired the masses with dreams of western ideals such as freedom, progress, and prosperity.

As Prime Minister Nehru has stressed (*see Reading No. 1*), Asians are no longer supine or submissive. They are dynamic and insistent upon the promises of independence. They are tragically impatient to leap across the centuries and achieve *now* what the rest of the world needed years or decades to accomplish. They will not allow their leaders the luxury of leisure, failure, or modest achievement. Revolution is their shibboleth. In Asia, which is usually described as phlegmatic, fatalistic, and unchanging, the clamor is for speed, speed, and more speed.

Together with real independence, Asians would stand on their self-respect; they would keep their dignity; they insist on equality. It might be called "face." They take new pride in themselves and in their heritage. They hold up to their youth the legendary figures of their history and glamorize their own artistic treasures and ancient civilizations. They will not be treated as second-class citizens, as stooges of the United States or Russia, or as human guinea pigs for nuclear explosions. They cannot help but resent the display of wealth which they associate with the west; and as long as "white men" live in their midst as kings or potentates, this will keep alive the atmosphere of resentment, seething anger, and recurring crisis.

Poverty. Economic disparity is at the root of internal, as well as external, problems. The native rich are as guilty as foreigners in the thoughtless or shameless display of wealth in the midst of poverty. There are only the rich and the poor, and a very few white-collar workers, business, and professional men who mark the beginning of a middle class. Poverty is everywhere. The small peasant farmer ekes scarcely enough from his land for food and clothing. If he ever gets any money, it goes for medicine, rents, taxes, repayment of loans, or for something from the village like cloth, salt, or a piece of candy for the children. A kerosene lamp, a bicycle, or a sewing machine is luxury.

As modern medicine brings its benefits and blessings, it reduces the death rate, lengthens the life span, prolongs the productive period, and cuts down infant mortality. Population increases faster than wealth, and Southeast Asia labors wearily to maintain its relative position on the economic treadmill. Even when the standard of living improves, the gap between the prosperity of the west and the east remains great.

Asians blame the west for their poverty. They overlook the benefits of imperialism—development, revenues, and social services—and see only its waste and abuses. To them imperialism meant hard work and starvation wages for the native population and fantastic profits and pensions for affluent westerners. It meant the end of local subsistence farming and the introduction of crop for export, such as sugar, copra, rubber, spices, tobacco, coffee, and tea. It subjected cottage industries to the competition of foreign-made consumption goods. It changed a comparatively self-reliant, individualistic farmer into a tiny, dependent, helpless cog in a gigantic alien economic system. The peasants and tenants remained poor, while landlords, traders, government bureaucrats, and aliens waxed rich.

The resentment against aliens includes Chinese and Indians as well as Europeans and Americans. Chinese dominate the economic activities of almost every city and village in Southeast Asia. They are the small traders, the shopkeepers, the miners, the plantation workers, the artisans, and the craftsmen; the rice-millers, the wholesalers, the bankers, the shippers, and the merchant princes. The natives, avoiding open competition with the Chinese, resort to nationalization and discriminatory legislation to increase their share in business and trade. The sentiment is that the Chinese will have to go.

The nations of Southeast Asia realize that they need the help of foreigners to rise above their poverty. Burma and Malaya need the British, the Philippines need the Americans, and Indonesia needs the Dutch. Capital, technical skill, and management talent from abroad are essential. Asians know that they must diversify and expand their agricultural production, and embark upon some kind of industrialization if they are to increase their exports, reduce their imports, and satisfy more of the consumption demands of their own people. But the lingering suspicions from the past are so compelling, that some leaders prefer *no* foreign aid to what they look upon as new imperialism in disguise. They pin their hopes of progress on state socialism or some form of economic nationalism. They have no fond memories of free enterprise, unlimited competition, or the capitalist system. They do not have an economic way of life which they are proud of nor a standard of living which they want to preserve. They have an environment of poverty which they seek to replace in the fastest and most thorough fashion possible.

Good Government. In the economic sphere, they want more of the good things of life; in the political sphere they cry for good government. They do not insist upon a western-style democracy nor a Russian-style dictatorship. By "good government" they mean one that will provide for a reasonable balance between an individual's demand for liberty and security and society's need for law and order. Good government is not peculiar to Europe; Asians have demonstrated their ability to create and operate successful institutions at every political level—local, provincial, and national.

Ideologies and forms mean little in Asia. Most Asians are accustomed to having decisions made for them, either by a local chief, a sultan, or someone in the provincial capital or the governor's palace. Local initiative is rare, and the habit has grown to look to the central government for everything from a rat-extermination campaign to the change of name of a village street. This is poor ground in which to sow the seeds of western-style democracy. Democracy needs training, experience, an educated and politically informed citizenry, a prosperous middle class and a healthy government budget. Rubber-stamp parliaments or rigged elections do not warrant the name "democracy." Some "democracies" provide neither human freedom nor social welfare.

As for communism, it is hardly the ideal answer to Asia's political perplexities. Indigenous cultural and religious patterns are antagonistic to communism. The subtleties of ideology are neither understood nor appreciated, and the ruthlessness of Communist discipline is cordially detested. Communism is often a meaningless label for simple, popular program which promises the party an opportunity for power.

Most of the contemporary leaders of Southeast Asia are men who have had the benefit of a western education and have risen to prominence on the issues of anti-imperialism and nationalism. They have little sympathy for communism, although they have not hesitated to cooperate with Communists as a matter of expediency. They know well enough that the Communists will turn against them whenever the time seems favorable. Their tactics should be to meet zeal with more zeal, to offer a better program and show a more favorable record than their Communists opponents.

Those responsible for the affairs of government must deal with problems which defy permanent or very satisfactory solutions. They are harassed by disgruntled members of their own party as well as by the opposition. They must have the necessary power if they are to govern well; at the same time they may not go against public will. If they would make the citizen be conscientious about his duties, they must respect his rights. They must remove the conditions which foster extremism, fanaticism, subversion, and anarchy. They must provide the military with arms, while they keep in check its political power. Above all they must handle public funds for the common good and not their own.

These are the things which Asians insist upon when they talk of good government. They want to achieve these objectives by adapting whatever forms they find suitable —and from all available sources—without regard for label or association.

Peace. In external affairs, the most popular slogan is peace. It is not that Southeast Asians are more devoted to peace or less inclined to war. Their history is a continuous chronicle of fighting; their heroes are usually men of war. In their behavior they are as volatile, pugnacious, and insistent upon their rights as any one else. The majority of male adults may seem contented to stay at home and work in peace, but there is no dearth of manpower for their large and well-trained armies. Southeast Asians have never shied away from soldiering or fighting. But modern war is something else again. It promises no benefit; it threatens only destruction. They want none of it.

Conscious of their own power vacuum, they have sought strength in the United Nations, its agencies, and in regional groupings. Nehru convened the first Asian Relations Conference in 1947, and the Colombo powers (Pakistan, India, Ceylon, Indonesia, and Burma) called the Asian-African conference at Bandung in 1955. Twenty-nine nations in attendance sought to speak with a common voice on economic and cultural cooperation, human rights and self-determination, problems of dependent peoples, and the promotion of world peace and cooperation. (*See Reading No. 2.*)

In search of "peace," one nation (North Vietnam) has chosen the side of Russia and Red China. Three (Thailand, the Philippines, and South Vietnam) have made common cause with the United States. Of these three, the first two have signed the Southeast Asia Collective Defense Treaty against aggression and subversion. (*See Reading No. 3.*)

The remaining nations in the region have refused to commit themselves to either side in the cold war. They insist that they are independent, not neutral, and that they contribute to "peace" by nonalignment with either military bloc. They would like to see the end of blocs, to have them supplanted perhaps by some Locarno-type arrangement in which both sides would join. They distinguish sharply between communism as an internal problem and Communist imperialism as an external menace. They see little to choose between Communist subtlety and anti-Communist intransigence as a producer of tension. They recognize the economic strength of the United States and the good points in its international record, but they tend to accept at face value Chou En-lai's five principles of mutual respect, nonaggression, noninterference, equality, and peaceful coexistence. They are courted by both sides, and they look to both sides for much needed aid and assistance.

The outside world can help all Southeast Asia, but it cannot provide the initiative, the energy, the enterprise, the self-sacrifice, and the devotion to public welfare required for an improvement in the position of Southeast Asia in today's world. These virtues must be cultivated by the people themselves. They would be independent; they must stand on their own feet. Otherwise, what meaning would there be to new freedom of which they are so fiercely proud?

A.D.	BURMA (PYUS) (MONES)	SIAM	CAMBODIA (KHMERS)	ANNAM (CHAMS) (ANNAMITES)	MALAY PENINSULA (PROTO- AND DEUTERO-MALAYS)	SUMATRA	JAVA
100				TONKIN			
200			FUNAN	(UNDER CHINA)	KEDAH		
300				CHAMPA	LANGKASUKA		
400			FUNAN CONQUERED				
500	SOUTHWARD DRIVE		BY KHMERS PRE-ANGKOR KHMER KINGDOM				
600	OF BURMANS						SAILENDRAS
700	PROME (PYU CAPITAL) CONQUERED SOUTHWARD DRIVE OF THAIS					SRIVIJAYA	
800			ANGKOR KINGDOM				MATARAM
900	PAGAN (BURMAN CAPITAL) FOUNDED PAGAN DYNASTY					UNION OF SAILENDRAS & SRIVIJAYA	
1000				TONKIN GAINS INDEPENDENCE			
1100	THATON (MON CAPITAL) TAKEN		WAR BETWEEN KHMERS & CHAMS				KADIRI
1200							
1300	MONGOL INVASION END OF PAGAN DYNASTY	THAI ESTABLISHED IN CHENGMAI	THAI ATTACKS	MONGOL INVASION	TAMERA LINGA	INVASION	SINGHASARI
1400	PEGU INDEPENDENT KINGDOM	THAI ESTABLISHED IN AYUTHIA	ANGKOR ABANDONED	MING CONQUEST ANNAM GAINS	MALACCA SIAMESE INVASIONS	CONQUEST OF SRIVIJAYA	MAJAPAHIT

2

CULTURE, COMMERCE, AND COLONIZATION

Southeast Asians, in studying their past, seek to understand the role of their own people in the great drama of human history. They are no longer satisfied with the dry chronicle of rulers and kings.

Indigenous Culture. Archaeological discoveries in Southeast Asia have produced pleistocene evidence of the earliest human forms on earth. The Java man is believed to have wandered the jungles thousands of years before the appearance, about twelve thousand years ago, of immigrants originating in the neighborhood of southwest China.

First came the Australoid-Veddoid types—ancestors of the hill tribes of Malaya and the Celebes and the Negritos of the Philippines—who were small and dark-skinned with woolly or wavy hair. Then came the Malay types now known as Indonesians—perhaps 2500 to 1500 B.C. —who were the forefathers of the Burmese, Siamese, Vietnamese, Malayans, island Indonesians, and Filipinos. There is no record of mass eviction or annihilation—just a continuing mixture of conqueror and conquered.

At the beginning of the Christian era, Indonesians cultivated the fields, knew the secrets of terracing and irrigation, domesticated the ox and the buffalo, enjoyed cockfights and pigfights and understood a rudimentary use of metals. They were excellent woodworkers, weavers, and pottery makers. They were seafarers and understood something of the stars. They lived in wooden houses and made clothing from the bark of trees. They were animists, and they worshipped their ancestors. They accorded women a favored place in their families, and they clustered their homes in villages. They gradually developed a body of laws and social customs.

19

Contacts with Other Asians. Southeast Asians were by no means savages when they felt the impact of Indian and Chinese civilizations. They were relatively advanced communities prepared to transform imported patterns into expressions of their own genius. They created the treasures of Borobudur, Angkor Wat, and Pagan—which were not mere imitations but were blends of native skills and alien ideas. For centuries Southeast Asia was a crossroads of culture and commerce.

From the time of Christ, Indian trading settlements existed in South Vietnam, Sumatra, Malaya, and Borneo. Traders, adventurers, and craftsmen were accompanied by priests and teachers who gradually developed centers of religious and cultural influence. Brahmanism and Buddhism—sometimes antagonistic, sometimes coexisting in peace—represented two different aspects of a single Indian civilization.

From the Indians, Southeast Asians received the new religions complete with temples, statues, philosophy, and mythology. They were taught the classical Sanskrit language and a new art of writing. They were given some knowledge of medicine and astrology. They were also introduced to superstitions and ceremonies which, in the light of modern education, were nonsensical and unsanitary.

Indian concepts of monarchy and law inspired the creation of Indianized states which represented political and commercial power in Southeast Asia for a millenium and a half, almost four times as long as the entire age of colonization. (*See Chart.*) Brahman rites appealed to potentates and aristocrats who could build monuments to themselves as incarnations of Hindu gods or devoted followers of the Lord Buddha. Indian inscriptions and Chinese chronicles perpetuate the memory of such states as Funan, Angkor, Srivijaya, Sailendra, and Majapahit.

Contacts with Chinese were as ancient and continuous as those with India. Chinese travellers, traders, artisans, warriors, and priests came by land and sea. They brought silk and incense, pottery and porcelain. They also brought their language and philosophy, their science and way of life. Chinese immigrants established themselves from the beginning as unbeatable economic competitors, but the

Chinese state confined its political ambitions to Annam (Vietnam). Some Southeast Asian courts for their own purposes recognized Chinese rights of investiture and tribute.

The arrival of Islam was comparatively recent. The faith was not acceptable until it was presented by Moslem merchants from India. Arabs were held in low esteem. Marco Polo told of only two Arab communities known in Sumatra in his day. By the end of the fifteenth century, when Arabs had gained control of the spice trade, twenty states in Sumatra, Java, and Malaya had adopted a synthetic blend of Mohammedanism as their religion. Many mosques were decorated with Hindu or Buddhist bas-reliefs. Local rulers accepted Mohammedanism (or Islam) because it symbolized wealth and commercial success. Common people simply followed the leader. Traders were effective missionaries, and the exchange of gifts and daughters proved more useful than the sword.

Malacca, founded in 1403 by a refugee from Singapore, became the center of Moslem influence. It grew into a trading mecca which was coveted by dying Majapahit and rising Siam. For its own protection, it paid handsome tribute money to China. Its fame spread to Europe, but its court fell victim to its own debauchery. Its cultural vitality survived. The Arabian language, Mohammedan romance, mysticism, and law spread from Malacca to the Moluccas—until challenged by new ideas and new forces from far beyond the seas.

Southeast Asia in 1500. Ordinary free men were mostly concerned with their families, with rice and fish, and with their farms and nets. They had industries: "mines, gold-washing, looms, farms, barter, naval construction, raising of poultry and stock, weaving of silk and cotton, distilleries, manufacture of arms, pearl fisheries, the civet industry, the horn and hide industry, etc.," according to Rizal. They paid their taxes and their tribute. They obeyed their chiefs and the customary law (the *adat*). They had faith in sorcery and magic and performed frequent rituals for their gods. The village was the ordinary limit of their horizons. Their lives were short, bittersweet compounds of pleasure and pain. They were pawns at the whim of kings or sultans.

As for the states of Southeast Asia, they were tiny, warring, personal, and despotic. Their interests were local; their problems were survival and succession to the throne. They were free from challenge of India or China. India was not yet unified, and China had retired into the shell of seclusion. Japan was practically unheard of. The Mongol invasions were bitter but half-forgotten memories.

Siam was ambitious, but enmeshed in wars. Burma was chaotic, and the Khmer kingdom of Angkor had disappeared. Annam was restless to expand in its new freedom. Malacca flourished, but it was surrounded by swamps and jungles which knew more of malaria and piracy than silver and gold. Sumatra and Java were mummies of a glorious past. Local sultans were ready to cooperate with any intruder. Hinduism and Buddhism had vanished except for Bali, crumbling monuments, and imperishable *wayang* tales. Islam was on the march and approached the southern islands of the Philippines. Life in the Philippines was enlivened with raids and punctuated by vendettas.

When America was discovered, Southeast Asia was already old. Culturally, its people were as complex as the Europeans who came to trade and remained to colonize.

Commerce and Colonization: Malaya. In 1511 the Portuguese captured Malacca and destroyed its Islamic character. They demolished mosques and mausoleums and used the stones for donjon towers. They built government houses and mansions, a cathedral and churches, barracks and a prison. They demanded workers and women. They swaggered by day and caroused by night. They fought pirates and smugglers and collected tolls and licenses from legitimate traffic. From their fortress headquarters and their ships at sea, they ran their precious monopoly of trade.

A long period of steady decline ended in 1641. The Dutch, with the help of Sumatrans and Malays from Johore, drove out the Portuguese. The Dutch continued their monopoly and, like the Portuguese, shied away from territorial control beyond Malacca. The Dutch position, in turn, was a casualty in the American Revolution and the Napoleonic wars against the British. The British East

India Company obtained Penang (*See Reading No. 4*), Malacca, and Singapore. (*See Reading No. 5.*) By a treaty which was signed in 1824 the British-Dutch spheres were divided into the Malay peninsula and the islands of Indonesia.

British interest in the three Straits Settlements suffered because of malignant disorders in the neighboring Malay states. Rival claimants to thrones fought and feuded; Chinese tin miners indulged in incessant quarreling. After 1874 one ruler after another was persuaded to enter into a treaty accepting a British resident, whose advice must be asked and followed in all matters save Malay custom and the Moslem religion. The British in exchange established law and order, maintained the sultan in his position, provided him with a steady income, and protected his state against all external dangers. The last of the treaties was not concluded until 1914, five years after the British territories of Malaya were rounded out by annexations from Siam. Great Britain guaranteed peace and the sanctity of contracts; while the boom in rubber brought prosperity to a complex foreign, Chinese, and Malay society.

Indonesia. The Spice Islands saw the Europeans at their worst—as pirates and butchers in spite of the veneer of Christian civilization. In 1602 the Dutch East India Company was established for commercial profit, but it was empowered to enter into treaties and agreements to build forts, establish governments, and maintain troops and law courts for the preservation of peace and order. It offered alliances to local chieftains and protection for Islam in exchange for help against the Portuguese and trading concessions. In 1611 it secured its monopoly in the Moluccas, and eight years later it established its capital at Batavia.

The company ruled in the Indies for two centuries. It extended its sway by wars, intervention in civil wars, and peaceful agreements. It operated through a system of indirect rule. Regents and local chiefs continued to govern, but they became vassals of the company. As such, they were made responsible for fixed annual deliveries of products. Dutch residents, assistant residents, and controllers remained in the background, but their heavy hands and eagle eyes were responsible for the profits of the company.

Chinese were imported for work in the fields or in the factories. As elsewhere, they prospered. They aroused the jealousy of the native Indonesians, and they incurred the hatred of the Dutch. Their status was always vulnerable and gave rise to frightful massacres.

As a result of the Napoleonic wars and the subsequent bankruptcy of the company, the Indies became wards of the Netherlands. They were administered by Sir Stamford Raffles during the British interlude (1811-1816) and exposed to the philosophy that their welfare was more important than Dutch profit. After the treaty of 1824, they were returned officially to the Dutch and made a monopoly of the crown.

In 1830 the Culture System, or production of export crops for net profit, was introduced. Java became a beautiful, huge plantation with increased production of all crops save rice for the peasant, who was neglected and subjected to new abuses. He was required to plant one-fifth of his arable land in export products and, in lieu of taxes, to work sixty-six days every year on government plantations. Exports from the Indies doubled imports, yet living levels remained among the lowest in Southeast Asia. The plight of the Indies was publicized in a stirring Dutch novel, *Max Havelaar,* and liberal spirits in the Netherlands were aroused.

The Agrarian Law of 1870 began an attack on the system of forced labor. It protected the peasants in their rice lands and opened unoccupied or uncultivated lands to private capital. Long-term leases were made available. Money poured into the Indies for agriculture and for industries as well. Technological and scientific advance was matched by increased efficiency in the administrative and judicial systems.

It was painfully clear that the native population was largely overlooked in the march of progress. The gap widened between the rich and the poor. Profits from new enterprises went to the Dutch—or to the Chinese. As a salve for the conscience and in the interest of justice, the throne announced a new Ethical Policy in 1901, dedicated to the improvement of native welfare. With new vigor, the Dutch set out to establish their authority over the last remaining defiant territories, sparing only British Borneo and Portuguese Timor.

Burma, Siam, and Indochina. These three countries were located off the monsoon trail, and their control was not vital for the fabulous trade in spices. They were more addicted to private wars than to commercial profits. For two centuries they were little affected by Europeans, other than colorful adventurers or missionaries.

In 1755 the kingdom of Burma was unified under Alaungapaya, but its fate was sealed in three nineteenth-century wars against the British. It became a colony of India as much as a colony of Great Britain. British influence dominated Rangoon, Mandalay, the Shan states, and Bhamo on the Burma road into China. British, Indian, and Chinese capital developed, at substantial profit, Burma's resources in rice, teak, mines, petroleum, and transport. Foreigners monopolized shipping, banking, and the public services.

In the seventeenth century, the rice-rich Siamese began the game of playing one power against another. They accepted French help to keep off the British and the Dutch. They learned to their regret of the imperialistic instincts of French missionaries, traders, and military experts. The Siamese then turned to a policy of seclusion. When the capital of Siam was moved to Bangkok (1768) and the Chakri dynasty founded (1782), the Siamese became more confident of their own strength. They renewed treaty relations with foreign countries and under Kings Mongkut (1851-1868) and Chulalongkorn (1868-1910) undertook a program of modernization and development. They lost great chunks of territory to the British and the French, but they salvaged their political independence.

In 1787 the King of Hue (in Indochina) ceded to France a base to Tourane and Poulo Condore (Condore Island) in exchange for assistance against his rival for the imperial throne of Annam. When he gained the throne, he sought the favor of China and expelled the French. Retaliation was delayed, but it was inevitable. All Indochina came under French rule although the forms of the empire were retained. A professional French army, with enlisted colonial personnel, maintained order;

French civil service, with lower echelons open to native talent, administered an uncompromising policy of assimilation; and French capital, augmented by Chinese, undertook timid exploitation of local resources.

The Philippines.   Unlike the rest of Southeast Asia, the Philippines immediately became the colony of its political overlord. The haughty Spanish conquistadores despised trade and manual labor; they came to conquer and rule. In 1519 the Indios—as they were called by the Spaniards—welcomed Magellan with rice, chickens, and fruit; after half a century they greeted Legaspi with swords and bamboo spears. Spanish arrogance turned hospitality into hostility, but Spain easily subdued the Indios, except the Moros, and placed its physical stamp on every city and town throughout the islands.

Manila was taken from the rajah in 1571. Its new prosperity depended upon taxes and tribute from the provinces, the commercial activity of the Chinese, and the annual galleon trade with Acapulco. The officials throttled all commerce except for their own gain. They slaughtered tens of thousands of Chinese and reduced the Indios to tenantry on the tremendous tracts of rice and sugar lands which were distributed to illustrados and friars. Native industries were abandoned or neglected as people were forced to build ships or man the oars as galley slaves. Population decreased as men were taken for costly wars or fruitless expeditions against the Dutch or the British. Manila was occupied for two years (1762-63) during the Seven Years War.

Native culture was despised. The Spaniards deigned to enrich it with their own blood, language, law, a single administrative system, and the Catholic church. Filipinos protested against the debasement of their spirit and the abuses of clericalism. Rizal wrote: "Every creature has its stimulus, its mainspring. Take it away from him and he is a corpse, and who seeks activity in a corpse will encounter only worms." In spite of Spanish concessions in the direction of liberalism, Filipinos rebelled on hundreds of occasions before 1896. By that time, just before the Americans came, the issue of colonialism in the Philippines was no longer a question of principle. It was only a matter of time.

				PORTUGUESE ADVENTURERS		
1500	1521. Magellan. 1571. Manila founded. Beginning of galleon trade to Acapulco.	Portuguese in the Spice Islands. 1577. Sir Francis Drake in Ternate. 1595. First Dutch ship arrived Bantam, Java.	1511. Portuguese base at Malacca.		Constant wars with Burma.	Wars of Unification. 1587. First visit of British.
1600	1603. Massacre of Chinese.	1601. British East India Company bases at Achin, Bantam. 1605. Dutch at Amboina. 1619. Dutch at Batavia. 1623. Dutch massacre at Amboina. 1682. English East India Company out of Indies.	1641. Dutch, under Gov. Van Diemen, took Malacca.	1620. French missionaries. 1664. French East India Company sought base.	1609. First Siamese visit to Europe. Dutch, British-French concessional trade. 1662. French missionaries. 1664. Dutch treaty. 1684. French treaty. 1688. French intrigue; seclusion policy.	Revival of power. British factory at Rangoon. Off and on trade until 1780. Dutch abandoned French trade and shipbuilding at Syriam.
1700	1762-3. Manila occupied by British.	Dutch power expanded. Dutch traders in Borneo. 1740. Massacre of Chinese. 1781-1784. Dutch trade monopoly destroyed. 1798. Dutch Government took over Dutch East India Company.	1786. British foothold in Penang.	1750. French-Annam treaty. 1787. Bishop of Adran activities in Annam.	1768. Capital established at Bangkok. 1782. Chakri Dynasty founded.	1755. Alaungpaya founded kingdom—lasted until ended by British.
1800	1810. Representation in *Cortes*. 1896. Rizal death. 1898. U. S. sovereignty.	1811. Raffles in Java. 1825-1830. Java wars. 1830. Culture system. 1848. Parliament interest in Colonial affairs. 1860. *Max Havelaar*. 1870. New agricultural policy. 1882. British North Borneo Co. charter.	1819. Singapore. 1824. BASIC BRITISH-DUTCH TREATY. 1862-72. Straits settlements organized. 1874. First British treaty with Malayan State. 1896. Federation.	1843. Revive French interest. 1862. French treaty: Annam and Cochin China. 1863. Cambodia Protectorate. 1867. Cochin China. 1884. French-Chinese treaty. 1887. Unification of French possessions. 1893. Laos Protectorate.	1826. British treaty. 1833. U. S. treaty. 1851-1868. King Mongkut. New treaties British, French, American. 1868-1910. Chula Long Korn. 1893. French treaty. 1896. French-British spheres of interest.	1826. First war against British. 1852. Second British war. 1885. Third British war. 1897. Became Provincial Gov't. China boundary fixed.
1900	1901. Civil Gov't. established. 1907. Legislative Assembly. 1916. Jones Law. 1935. Commonwealth. 1946. Independence.	1901. Ethical policy. 1918. Volksraad. 1926-7. Nationalist uprisings. 1945. Independence.	1909. Northern States form Siam. Federal council established. 1914. Johore treaty. 1946. Union. 1948. Federation. 1957. Merdeka.	1945. Vietnam independent. 1954. Laos and Cambodia independent.	1904. French treaty. 1907. French treaty. 1909. British treaty—Malay states for extraterritoriality. 1922. New treaties exemplified by U. S. treaty.	1937. Separated from India. 1948. Independent.

3

EMERGING NATIONS

Southeast Asians felt the full force of colonialism during the closing years of the nineteenth century. Empires replaced trading companies. Raw materials and markets for industrial products became more important than trade. The faint beginnings of the age of science—steamships, cable, telegraph, and railways—shook the foundations of native society.

Great forces generated strong counterpressures. Peoples became increasingly aware of their wretchedness. An articulate elite sparked rebellion against unkind native traditions, and eventually against foreign masters. Bright young students took to heart the lessons they learned about the British parliament and the French Revolution. They liked particularly the American Declaration of Independence and absorbed their ideas of revolution and progress from the inspiration and models of the west.

Reforms came too slowly for impatient spirits. Small and weak as the embryo nations of Southeast Asia were, they took encouragement from their formidable Asian neighbors. India formed the Congress Party and unleashed the *swaraj* campaign; China experienced the Boxer rebellion, the birth of the Kuomintang, and the republican revolution; and Japan won an unbelievable Asian military victory over the Russian colossus. Japan's ultranationalism became a beacon light for all Asians who would throw off the colonial yoke.

Then President Wilson dazzled Southeast Asians with his electric message of self-determination, and the Russian revolution added a new impetus to social change. Lenin linked the demand of subject peoples for self-government with his anticapitalist campaign for world revolution. He declared that the road to victory in the west lay through the east. Nationalists worked with socialists and

Communists before World War II and used the tragedies of the great depression of 1930-1932 to strengthen their program and their leadership.

Each country pursued its separate course to nationhood and independence without much cooperation or cross-fertilization of ideas from its neighbors. Siam's problems were internal, since it had no external sovereign to displace. The Philippines, after its first skirmishes against Spain, had comparatively an easy time against the Americans. Burma, Indonesia, and Indochina found little sympathy for nationalist aspirations in the hearts of their masters. Malaya slumbered a long time before it was disturbed by dreams of independence.

Siam. Thanks to the modernization program of its enlightened kings, Siam led its neighbors in the process of making a modern nation. The last treaty by which Siam lost territory was also the first by which it regained some of its surrendered sovereignty: in exchange for the Siamese states in Malaya, Great Britain gave up its rights to extraterritoriality in Siam. The United States and European nations followed the British lead.

In 1932 a western-trained cabal of civil servants and military officers engineered a palace coup which indicated the direction in which Siam's leaders intended to proceed. The common people were not involved. A young law professor, variously known as Luang Pradit or Pridi Banomyong, teamed up with a military man, Phibun Songgram, to force the king to grant a constitution. The constitution provided for a council of ministers and a peoples' assembly. On the economic front, the successful conspirators demanded nationalization, industrialization, and the end of the Chinese stranglehold on all of the local business.

There was no communism, no violent anti-foreignism. Foreign advisers were continued in their jobs. In foreign policy, Siam determined to pursue an independent course toward aggressive Japan. Siam had its grievances against the west and hoped that Japan might offer an aid program including a canal across the Isthmus of Kra. Japan's influence would be valuable for the recovery of lost territories. In 1939 Siam changed its name to the more nationalistic "Thailand," and in 1942 it joined forces with

Japan in declaring war against the United States and Great Britain.

The Philippines. The long history of Spanish domination gave the Philippines a unique consciousness of solidarity and provided the Filipinos with a persistent target. Spanish concessions never matched Philippine demands. In 1872 a serious revolt occurred in Cavite Province, and three priests were garroted for advocating the appointment of native parish priests. In 1896 the heroic death of the gentle Rizal before a Spanish firing squad ended the effort for reform with the law. (*See Reading No. 6.*) Fiery revolutionists welcomed the American war against Spain, but they felt cheated when the occupation of Manila failed to bring independence.

Filipinos were treated liberally by the American regime. They were given all the guarantees of the American Bill of Rights except trial by jury and the right to bear arms. Their system of government was to be designed for "the happiness, peace, and prosperity of the people of the Philippines." (*See Reading No. 7.*) Measures by which Filipinos were to be ruled were to be made to conform "to their customs, their habits, and even to their prejudices."

By 1907 a popularly elected legislative assembly was created, and a Nacionalista party was launched. Filipinos were given more legislative authority and more jobs in the civil service. In 1916 they were promised independence as soon as stable government could be established, and in 1934 that promise was implemented by Act of Congress. A commonwealth form of government was set up for ten years, after which complete independence was to follow.

Benevolent legislation did not settle the practical problems of independence. Bitter feuding slackened off, and political speeches became less vitriolic. Americans were uneasy about their heritage of democracy. The Philippine Constitution of 1935—the oldest in Southeast Asia—provided for the forms and philosophy of democracy. Government in action was a travesty of democracy. A party machine, or a single dynamic leader, controlled elections, appointments, and spoils. The same small oligarchy controlled politics and economic power. The Philippines were not prepared economically for independence. The feudal system of land tenure produced continuous agrarian unrest, and commercial prosperity depended upon free trade with the U. S. Domestic economy faced impending crisis and aggravated political dissatisfaction. Only the Japanese invasion silenced a campaign for "re-examination."

Burma and Indonesia. After Burma's pacification, a system of direct rule was inaugurated, headed by a British governor and manned by British civil servants. The traditional patterns of feudal allegiance and customary law were replaced by district commissioners and village tract headmen who were primarily concerned with the cold administration of Indian law and British justice.

British rule brought undeniable benefits. Public funds were used for public purposes. Commercialized rice production on a tremendous scale was introduced into Lower Burma. Transportation was improved and natural resources were carefully exploited. Business enterprises expanded from rice milling, timber, and operation of river boats to petroleum, mining, and small factories. Burma's villagers shared little in the prosperity because aliens reaped the profits. Indians and Chinese even supplied most of the labor.

In spite of legal controls, economic and social life disintegrated. Debts increased, agrarian distress grew, and litigation and crime multiplied. Buddhist monasteries, centers of stability, lost their reputation for moral leadership and enlightenment. Some became centers for operations of dacoits or bandits. In 1906 the Buddhists organized a Young Men's Buddhist Association, and in 1919 a general council of Buddhist Associations which agitated for home rule.

The British took guarded steps in the direction of self-government, but they retained control of foreign affairs, defense, finance, and minorities. The bureaucrats contributed indirectly to general uneasiness. They stressed such matters as administrative standards, economy of expenditure, incorruptibility of the police and courts, and neglected such problems of vital interest to Burmans as tenancy, rent control, land alienation, and limitation of Indian immigration. In 1930 the price of rice dropped, taxes continued, Indian money-lenders called in loans and foreclosed mortgages. The habit of lawlessness was too much. Riots broke out which assumed an anti-British complexion.

After the separation of Burma from India in 1935, the nationalist movement accelerated. New political leaders resorted to old practices like favoritism and bribery and built up large personal followings. The political scene was energized by a Dobama Asiayone (We Burmans Association), or Thakin party. Young students who insisted on the right to be called the respectful term of Thakin (or Mister) denounced corruption and took their stand four-square for nationalism. They did not turn their backs on Buddhism or western technology. They resorted to strikes, and some made common cause with the Burma Communist Party and the Freedom Bloc, both of which were organized in 1939. When they failed to get satisfaction from the British, some thirty of their leaders went to Japan for further training. They returned as guides and interpreters with the invading Japanese army in 1942.

Indonesia had an equally checkered struggle for nationhood. Resistance against the Dutch was as old as Dutch hegemony, but it was a long time before revulsion against poverty and ignorance became a protest against colonialism. Raden Adjeng Kartini, a lovely woman who died in childbirth in 1904 at the age of twenty-five, was one of the first to articulate the unexpressed longings of her people for advancement through the medium of Dutch education. In 1908 *Budi Utomo* (Beautiful Endeavor) welfare society and a union of railway and tramway workers were organized. Three years later, *Sarekat Islam* (Islamic Association), whose common bond was religion and opposition to the Chinese, called for progress towards nationalism under the Dutch flag. A radical element failed to gain control of this organization and in 1920 broke away to found the PKI or the "Party Kommunist of Indonesia," the oldest Communist party in Southeast Asia.

The Dutch could not ignore the rising tide. They promised a Volksraad, or representative legislature at the national level, and they deleted from the Constitution the reference to the Indies as a colony. Many Dutch sympathized with Indonesians, and many Indonesian students went to the Netherlands, where they inevitably championed the cause of their homeland. Poverty was their chief grievance. Had the prewar national income been distributed among Indonesians alone, the per capita annual income would have amounted to only seventeen American dollars. Little wonder that students and workers came under the influence of left-wing socialism and communism. The Dutch government could not distinguish between Nationalists and Communists, and during the strikes of 1926 arrested some 13,000 as disturbers of the peace. Of these, nearly one-third were imprisoned, and one in ten was sent into exile. The PKI was outlawed, and a new PNI or "Party Nationalist of Indonesia" came into prominence.

Sukarno became a national figure as early as 1927. He was a young engineering student and a member of the Bandung study club. He helped to organize the PNI, and he changed his beliefs gradually from cooperation with the Dutch to non-cooperation. He placed a great deal of faith in the "wild schools," so called because they were free from the restraints of official dictation. Early in the thirties, the Dutch determined there should be no revolutionary mass action. They dissolved the PNI and sent Sukarno, Hatta, and Sjahrir—among others—into exile. (*See Reading No. 8.*)

The agitation continued. Indonesians protested against poor jobs and low wages, discrimination in the civil service, and lack of educational opportunity. The Dutch consented to cautious moves towards self-government but not towards independence. They opened more jobs to Indonesians and extended the prerogatives of the Volksraad. The pace of economic reforms slowed down, due to world conditions. When the depression struck, the Indies were unable to get significant help from the mother country. Indonesians and the Dutch in the Indies tended to pool their energies and make common cause for recovery. This separation of interests was accentuated by the Nazi blitzkrieg in the Netherlands and the Japanese occupation of the Indies. These events brought new complications to the inchoate, but formulating, demands of the Indonesians for independent nationhood; and Indonesians, under a Japanese invader's heel, were far from satisfied with the promise of the queen that after the war the Indies would be given dominion status in a world-wide Dutch commonwealth.

Indochina and Malaya.   The lag of nationalism in Indochina was partially due to divergent local interests. Annamese from Tongking to Cochin-China had a common culture, but they were distinct from the peoples of Cambodia, Laos, and the hill tribes. The Annamese were poor, disease-ridden and often hungry. In a bad year in the north, many peasants lost their tiny farms and migrated to tenancy in the south. Desperation forced them to leave the security that lay in their family ties and their village communities. Half a million Chinese in Indochina cared little for nationalism. They were inclined to maintain their ties with China, and to cooperate wherever necessary with Annamese or French in order to protect their own economic position. Whatever unity existed in Indochina was the product of common resistance to French lethargy, cynicism, and poor administration.

The main reason for the slow development of the spirit of nationalism was the lack of people who knew or cared. The emperor might have served as a rallying point, but he did not. The masses were inert, uninformed, and without hope; the mandarinate was active, but individualistic and divided in their loyalties. These men, functionaries of the Court or the French, were children of the well-to-do and were educated in western knowledge and western values. They had a little power but not enough. The French limited their opportunities and never gave them responsibilities commensurate with their talents. They were frustrated and dissatisfied. These people—of the stamp of Ngo Dinh Diem—were anti-Marxist and preferred their nationalism undiluted with socialism or communism. They disliked the discipline of organization, and they were easy targets for the efficient French police.

The nationalist idea found new life and support in the thousands of coolies who went to dig trenches in France in World War I. The most outstanding personality was Ho Chi Minh, son of a mandarin, who was born about the same time as Chiang Kai-shek. He worked as a ship steward, photographer's assistant, and assorted odd jobs. At the Conference of Versailles, he insisted upon self-determination for Indochina. Then he joined the French Communist Party. He was an old hand at the Communist game before he went to Moscow. In 1925 he organized the Vietnamese Youth outside of their homeland, and in 1930 he organized the Communist Party in Indochina. His stormy career took him in and out of Russia, China, Southeast Asia, and bourgeois jails. His philosophy was a blend of nationalism and communism, and it found expression in the formation of the Vietnam Independence League, or the Viet Minh, on the eve of the Japanese invasion.

Nationalism was even tardier in Malaya than in Indochina. The reasons were prosperity and pluralism. The awkward British administration of Straits Settlements, Federated States, and Unfederated States provided a tolerable method of adapting a medieval structure to the demands of the twentieth century. Sultanates were obliged to concern themselves not only with smuggling and piracy but also with malaria control, reforestation, education, and the world price of rubber and tin. The British provided an honest and reasonably efficient government under which all races could live and work. Political agitators, including the Communists, usually received their funds and inspiration from the outside and were not able to produce much real demand either for independence or more self-government.

It was generally feared that any change in the status quo might aggravate the religious, racial, economic, and political problems of Malaya's plural society. There was a feeling that the slightest incident might disturb the surface harmony. The Malay States contained a slight majority of Malay peoples; Singapore was overwhelmingly Chinese. As long as the Malay States and Singapore were administered separately, neither majority was jeopardized. Union would mean an over-all Chinese majority. The Malays feared and distrusted the Chinese. Malays sleep in the noonday sun; Chinese work until midnight. Malays were loyal to a sultan and the Moslem religion. They looked down upon Chinese and Indians as infidels and unbelievers. As people of the country, Malays regarded

Chinese and Indians as transients, without loyalty to
Malaya, eager only to make a fortune and go home.
Chinese and Indians were inclined to hold Malays in
contempt. These attitudes were getting worse. Educated
Malays became more anti-Chinese. More Chinese tended
to set up permanent homes in their adopted country
and demanded a better status. As Victor Purcell described
the condition: "Time, though smiling, was in labor and
a political hydra was in her womb."

After four centuries of colonialism, the fate of imperial
powers in Southeast Asia was foreshadowed before World
War II. Gracefully or forcefully, they would surrender
the right to rule distant lands and different peoples. New
nations would come into existence, which would build
upon their ancient past and the contributions of their
recent masters. The preparation for independence was im-
perfect, but the right was undeniable. The new nations
were not psychologically ready for a Greater East Asia
Co-Prosperity Sphere (*see Reading No. 9*), but they
welcomed Japan's promise of liberation. War brought
demoralization and destruction, but it marked the transition from the old negative attitude of opposition to the
new, positive determination to forge ahead. National
movements, already in mid-stream, would drop their
foreign pilots and take command of their own ships of
state.

— 4 —

INDONESIA

A survey of Southeast Asia since World War II begins with its largest and most populous area—Indonesia.

Japanese Occupation. The wartime fate of Indonesia was sealed by the fall of the Netherlands. The wealth of the Indies was diverted to Japan, first by diplomacy and then by conquest. The Japanese took Batavia in March, 1942, and occupied all the major islands. Little fighting was required, and only slight damage was inflicted. The Japanese moved too fast for a scorched earth policy to be entirely effective. Three centuries of Dutch dominion came to an inglorious end in a moment.

Indonesians were bewildered but far from free. They felt the heel of a new master, who advertised himself as the Savior, the Leader, and the Light of Asia. For a brief time, Indonesians regarded Japan as the most advanced nation in Asia: strong, efficient, and well intentioned. Then the awakening came. Japan wanted Indonesia for itself, for its own victory. Ships and troops poured into Indonesia; administrators and propagandists came with them. To the Indonesians, the Japanese had seemed liberators from the Dutch. Good will towards the Japanese evaporated when they seized the meager food supplies, conscripted labor, and took precious petroleum, bauxite, nickel, and rubber in exchange for worthless currency.

The common people suffered most. The young and the healthy were drilled to exhaustion under the boiling sun. They were regimented and spied upon; they were beaten for trivial offenses and cast into prisons. They were jobless and starved. The native elite was disillusioned quickly and asked for independence, but Japan hedged. The red and white flag of Indonesia was banned, and political discussions were tabooed. Indonesia was treated like a military camp until the tide of war changed. Then Japan

curried the favor of Indonesians and brought them into
the administration. On March 1, 1945, a committee was
created to inquire into, and to prepare for, independence.

Excitement ran high. Indonesians gained new self-con-
fidence as independence approached. They received encouragement from the Japanese, who preferred a free
Indonesia to the return of the Dutch. Before the Japanese
surrender, the Indonesians formulated the philosophy of
the new State. (*See Reading No. 10.*) While the Dutch
planned to re-establish their rule, the Indonesians developed their ideas for one nation, one language, and
one people. They proclaimed their independence on
August 17, 1945, five days before the people knew of
the Japanese defeat. Sukarno, Hatta, and Sjahrir were the
great popular heroes. The fiery, likeable Sukarno was
the living symbol of victorious nationalism.

Fighting for Independence. For six weeks of bed-
lam, the Indonesians made the most of their independence. Their own armies were symbols of authority. On
September 29, 1945, British troops entered Indonesia to
disarm and repatriate 213,000 Japanese and to protect
200,000 Dutch internees. The British, with the Dutch,
asked cooperation of the new republican government.
Mutual restraint and understanding were impossible, and
Batavia became a bloody battlefield. Murder and arson
spread throughout Java, and the struggle crystallized into
a war between independence and the return of colonialism. After a year of chaos incarnate, the Dutch—largely
aided and equipped by Americans—re-established control
over sullen, determined guerrillas who fought with spears
and bamboo. That year gave the temper of hardened
steel to Indonesian nationalism.

On March 25, 1947, the Dutch and the Indonesians
accepted a formula which recognized the authority of the
Indonesian Republic in Java and Sumatra. The Outer Islands were to be administered separately but joined with
the Indonesian Republic to form the United States of Indonesia—which in turn would be part of the Dutch Commonwealth. This arrangement broke down in three
months. On July 19, 1947, the Dutch initiated their first
police action. It was a losing battle, both against the Indonesians and against world opinion. Pressure from the

United Nations forced a new truce agreement, signed aboard the American cruiser Renville. Peace and profit eluded the Dutch. They could not reopen their business houses, and they could not even live in safety with their families. Homes were burned, plantations destroyed, and exports were wiped out. The last ties of friendship turned into hatred. The Communists increased their hold on Indonesian politics, and they launched, in September, 1948, at Madiun, an abortive attempt to seize power. The Dutch tried a second futile police action in December, 1948, and then resigned themselves to negotiations for salvage. The Round Table Agreements of The Hague, December, 1949, marked the formal end of the Dutch empire in the Indies and the transfer of their sovereignty over all but West Irian to the new state of Indonesia. Indonesia was admitted into the United Nations in June, 1950.

People and Parties. On August 17, 1950, after five years of nominal independence, Indonesia proclaimed its provisional constitution. Popular excitement ran high, but an entire decade of destruction and devastation, of war and revolution is a cruel prelude to a new experiment in statehood. The government was to be a unified republic, with a president, a cabinet, and a legislature. Sukarno kept the presidency, and the self-constituted Central National Committee assumed the role of the National Assembly.

As elsewhere, the responsibility for government and administration fell upon the shoulders of a small group of men. Some of their names and characters were well known: as Sukarno, Hatta, Sjahrir, Natsir, Ali, and Djuanda. The whole group did not consist of more than a few thousand, and its central core could be counted in hundreds. Most were Dutch-educated and Dutch-speaking. They inherited the age-old tradition of authority, but they were without top-level administrative experience. They were not wealthy. They had no connections with landlords, as the oligarchy in the Philippines, and no direct stake in the capitalist system. They tended to equate capitalism and colonialism. They were socialists of the intellectual variety, not Communists; they were incapable of the bread-and-butter approach, which would have capturcd the peasants and workers. They were as alien to the masses as the Dutch. They allotted and re-allotted among themselves the best jobs in the government, armed forces, political parties, and private enterprise. Within this elite, political factions formed and broke off, with disastrous effects on the life span of cabinets. National unity was sapped by envy, jealousy, intrigue, and suspicion.

Party organizations mushroomed. All were nationalistic and socialistic, and all but the Communists were neutralists. Beyond that the lines of division were not clear cut. The PNI or Party-Nationalist-Indonesia continued as the rallying point for the fanatical nationalists. They found it difficult to agree on a positive course of action after their prime objective had been achieved. They were free but bewildered. Both Sukarno and Hatta detached themselves from the party, and placed themselves above partisanship. Those Indonesians who used either Moslem religion as the basis of political action could not agree on a single party, even to check the Communist infidels. The Masjumi, or Council of Indonesian Moslem Associations—created in 1943 for a united front against the Japanese—tended to be liberal in its political and social views. The N.U., Nahdatul Ulama or Association of Islamic Scholars, was more orthodox and conservative and was popular among the small businessmen and the peasants. Curiously enough, it was more disposed than the Masjumi to cooperate politically with the nationalists and the Communists. Another Moslem group, Dar-ul-Islam, consisted of the extremists, who advocated an out-and-out Moslem state. They sheltered guerrillas and bandits and permitted their movement to degenerate into sheer terrorism. The Catholic party never attracted more than a slight following, and the Socialists, in their intellectual snobbery, lost even their early following. The PKI, the Party Kommunist of Indonesia, grew rapidly and took its policy cues from Moscow or Peking. A small proletarian party, called the Partai Murba, followed the Communist line internally but refused to bow to foreign direction.

Government in Action. With such a small reservoir of talent so badly divided, the archipelago was wracked by political instability. Weak coalition cabinets rose and fell, and administration deteriorated. The elite was not accustomed to the self-imposed forms of democracy. New blood did not have the spirit of self-sacrifice which was the birthright of the first generation of freedom fighters. It was difficult to shift from the time-honored techniques of opposition to the techniques of rapid decision-making required by a party in power. Blundering and inefficiency gave way to bribery and corruption. No political machinery seemed capable of motion unless lubricated with rupiahs. The outer islands complained about Java. They thought their own men—Bataks, Bugis, Minangkabaus, or Balinese—were more capable than Javanese. They resented the pay and the privileges of the Javanese bureaucracy. They wanted their own islands to benefit from their export earnings. For example, Sumatra received only 10 per cent of the national budget, but it contributed 75 per cent of the national export.

The outer islands did not wish to destroy the unity of the state. They wanted more autonomy in administration. They demanded further decentralization. Army officers with strong local ties were most insistent, and they were politically powerful. Under the Dutch, the army became strong. It was well paid and staffed largely by Christian Amboinese. After the war, the guerrillas took over the ranks. The old-line officers, well disciplined, resisted nascent political interference; but the politicians and the common soldiers found joint interests in ultra-nationalism and near-communism.

The Communists took on new life, perhaps from China, after the Madiun incident. In 1951 Sukarno imposed curbs on the Communists and three years later warned them against going too far. Then the Communists in Indonesia shifted their tactics along with Communists throughout the world. They renounced rebellion for peaceful conversion of peasants, labor, soldiers, students, youth, and women. They built a strong grass-roots organization and campaigned openly and peacefully for members. Their propaganda took the form of such practical measures as distributing free medicine for victims of the Asiatic flu. They were careful not to offend the sensibilities of the Moslems, never referring to religion as the opiate of the people nor criticizing Moslem leaders.

They helped to build mosques and interrupted their political meetings when it was time for the call to prayer. They set out to demonstrate that they could operate constitutionally in times of peace, as well as subversively in times of crisis. They declared that while they were friendly to both Peking and Moscow, they were servants of neither. They clothed their program with phrases like "peace," "nationalism," and "cooperation against the imperialists." As long as they refrained from violence, the government was happy enough.

Double, Double, Toil and Trouble. Political "diversity" was bad enough, but economic and social problems were infinitely worse. If anything, poverty increased. Agriculture—70 per cent of the economic life of Indonesia—suffered most. Peasant farmers could not produce enough to eat. Almost a million tons of rice per year were needed to feed hungry mouths. Farm productivity failed to reach prewar levels. Debts increased, and, without Dutch protection, tiny family farms were further subdivided or sold to landlords. The price index in rural areas doubled between 1950 and 1955.

Plantations were abandoned when leases expired, or were left at the mercy of squatters. The agricultural benefits of years of scientific management were dissipated. Export products fluctuated wildly in value, depending upon the foreign buyers. Smuggling outstripped legitimate trade. Shipping, of vital necessity to the Archipelago, was in the hands of the Dutch, but its status became increasingly precarious.

The situation in industry was equally dark. The nationalists were surprised when nationalism failed automatically to bring prosperity. They underestimated the damaging effects of their treatment of Dutch investments, and they failed to realize that their talk of nationalization and socialization would frighten away the local Chinese, as well as foreign investors. Companies with heavy investments in Indonesia undertook grave risks when they modernized or expanded existing plants and equipment. Heavy taxes and exchange restrictions handicapped private enterprise. There was a 15 per cent tax on sales, 52 per cent on profits, and 66 per cent on dollars sent out. Imports were permitted only if certificates would show an equivalent in exports. If the manager of an oil company wanted to buy an electric refrigerator for his home, he had to show that he had set aside the price equivalent in foreign sales. Endless forms slowed up and complicated every process of trade. Labor was not inclined to work and developed more and more antipathy towards working for foreigners. To individual brigandage and thievery were added organized idleness and sabotage.

Indonesia wanted industrial growth and expansion, but it was hard pressed to stop its plunge towards bankruptcy. It operated on a chronic budget deficit and squandered its accumulated reserves. On the black market, its currency brought only a fraction of the official rate. As its real income shrank, it talked of saving 6 per cent for the five-year period to 1960 and hoped for savings of 15 per cent by 1975. It produced plans for expansion in agriculture, mining, and industry, power and irrigation, transportation and social services, but it must be added that the only reality in its industrial planning was that contributed by foreign grants, loans, and trade agreements. The United States, the United Nations, the World Bank, some nations of the Colombo Plan, the Netherlands, and Russia contributed substantially to Indonesia.

Economic confusion aggravated deep-seated social problems. Farmers were moved to new fury by tax collectors and landlords and even began to ask embarrassing questions about rich sultans. Men and women in small villages—through their enormously expanded schools—learned of teachers and doctors in the cities, and wanted the same. Better health, improved housing, better working conditions, and more help from the government were viewed as rights. The government opened schools and taught the national language with real energy. It could not escape the social demands which came with education. Much of modern Indonesia continued to live as it had in the sixteenth century; but a large part of its society began slowly to move into new channels. The momentum of eighty million people in flux became the determinant factor in Indonesia's future.

Foreign Affairs. With so many problems at home, Sukarno characterized his foreign policy as anti-colonial, peaceful coexistence, and adherence to the moral principles of the constitution. His touchiness on the colonial issue caused him to reject for three years American overtures for economic assistance. He used West Irian as a battle cry against the Dutch but stated that he had no legal claims to British Borneo or Portuguese Timor. He said communism and democracy can coexist, but colonialism and peace cannot. He dissolved the union with the Dutch, dismissed the Dutch military mission, and denounced unilaterally all economic and financial agreements.

West Irian is a country of 160,000 square miles, with a population of 700,000, only half of whom have been brought under administrative control. Legal arguments between the Dutch and Indonesians were of less consequence to the world than the bitterness between the two peoples. In Indonesia, the West Irian Liberation Movement inspired demonstrations and riots. Mobs spattered paints on foreign cars and buildings, and daubed trees and walls with "Kill the Dutch," or "Dutch get out" signs. Indonesians boycotted the Dutch, took over their business enterprises, closed their consulates and ordered the fifty thousand passport holders to leave their country. Indonesian diplomats warned that Dutch insistence on self-determination for the West Irians could lead to "the disintegration of the Indonesian state, the end of our active independent policy and also of our present democratic character."

Sukarno adopted a moderate tone in matters of less immediate diplomatic importance to him. He spoke of injecting the voice of reason into world affairs, and of mobilizing all the spiritual, all the moral, all the political strength of Asia and Africa on the side of peace. Identified as a leader of the Afro-Asian bloc and a spokesman for neutralism, he insisted that he was not neutral, but "independent and active." He visited the United States but did not show the same enthusiasm he displayed when he visited Jugoslavia, China, and Russia. In Moscow he received an imperial welcome. He was quartered in the Kremlin, given an honorary degree, and provided with an audience of a hundred thousand people at his speech in the Lenin Stadium. When he received the Russian president on a return visit in 1957, he took "the wonderful old man" on a political barnstorming tour of the islands. With regard to China, Sukarno said he was impressed with their unity and their improved standard of living. He and his entire party of forty thought that China was "a happier, freer country than the U.S.S.R."

Partially because of the possibilities of the 1,500,000 Chinese minority in his own country, Sukarno followed a cautious policy towards China. He refused to vote against the United Nations resolution condemning China's action in Korea, and he endeavored to conclude a citizenship treaty with Chou En-lai. The Chinese embassy in Djakarta is the embassy of Peking, not of Formosa. The news about China which Chinese read in Indonesian papers, or in Chinese papers in Indonesia, was of the "happy, free" variety, and never as interpreted by the enemies of the Chinese Communists. Sukarno considered himself as a sincere, loyal member of the United Nations, willing to cooperate with all regardless of social systems. He made his peace with Japan, and said that he wanted the greatest possible help for his people in trade, commerce, technical development, and national social reconstruction.

The Guided Democracy.   The first national elections in Indonesia in 1955 gave the Nationalists and the Masjumi about 20 per cent each of the 38,000,000 votes cast and the seats in the 263-member National Assembly. The NU, or Moslem Scholars, received about 18 per cent of the votes, while the Communists got slightly less (16 per cent). Elections for a constitutional assembly returned approximately the same proportions. No party was in a decisive position; the political machine was without a chauffeur; Sakarno took the wheel in his own hands. On February 21, 1957, he announced a new concept of government. (*See Reading No. 11.*) He proclaimed a state of war and siege and the substitution of mutual agreement for majority rule. Away with outmoded democracy and bickering parties! Government would be turned over to a national advisory council, made up of workers, Nationalists, Communists, peasants, etc., and a cabinet of experts praised Sukarno's drastic action. Hatta and the Moslem parties objected. They feared that Sukarno had acted in haste. On April 17, a new cabinet took office. Eighteen members took their oath as a turbaned mullah held a pocket size Koran over their heads; three Protestants and one Catholic swore on the Bible; the last lone independent took his pledge without benefit of holy writ. The cabinet's job was to stamp out rebellion, shore up the national economy, break the last ties with the Dutch and establish a strong, central government.

In spite of hopeful words, the crisis persisted. The economic situation showed no signs of improvement, and the Communists registered significant gains in local elections. On August 17, 1957, Sukarno delivered another address which he called "Year of Decision." (*See Reading No. 12.*) He argued more fervently than ever for the end of chatterbox democracy, and for the national dedication to a new life. His pleas could not disguise his difficulties. He made concessions to Hatta to attract him back into the government; he conducted talks with the colonels who controlled the outlying islands. Military victory over rebels in Sumatra and the Celebes only served to aggravate his woes. He still had to convince his people that his guided democracy was a genuine and not a "corruptionist-Communist" alliance or a thinly guised dictatorship. No scheme of government—no matter how sincere or ingenious—could in itself cure the nation's internal ills nor gain its external objectives.

— 5 —

MALAYA AND SINGAPORE

It is only a step from Indonesia, the largest country in Southeast Asia, to Malaya, the smallest country. On the threshold of Malaya is the island of Singapore, the last colony in Southeast Asia to become an independent state.

Malaya Under the Japanese. In the opening days of the war, the Japanese made incredible "face" by sinking the mighty British battleships *Repulse* and the *Prince of Wales*. In fifty-five days, Japanese troops overran Malaya and reduced the "impregnable" fortress of singapore. According to Sir Richard Winstedt, the last regiment to quit the mainland was the Argyll and Sutherland Highlanders. A remnant of 200 out of 850 men crossed the causeway with pipes playing Blue Bonnets over the Border. It was "one of those gestures which bring tears of pride to the eyes and create a nation, but which generally should bring tears of shame for lives thrown away." Japanese newsreels showed endless lines of prisoners of war and a poignant unconditional surrender. General Yamashita said, "I want no fancy words—just a simple 'yes' or 'no.' "

Malaya and Singapore suffered the usual hardships of occupation. The four northern states were restored to Thailand, and the residual territory, plus Sumatra, was administered as a single military government. Singapore in particular was too valuable to be given independence. The Malays were induced to collaborate in their easygoing way. They were placed in jobs with good pay and imposing titles, but with no responsibility or power. Some Chinese were shot as supporters of Chiang Kai-shek, others were beaten and taxed. Some made fortunes on the black market. Survival depended upon their extraordinary genius for adaptability. The Indians were

47

utilized for the Indian Independence League, the Indian National Army, and the Free Indian Government. One outstanding Communist, Loi Tek, proved to be a thorough scoundrel, and another, Chin Peng, led the guerillas. In 1943 he organized a Malay Peoples Anti-Japanese Army (MPAJA) with a nine-point Communist program. In recognition of his wartime service to the British, he was flown to London to participate in the victory parade. Neither nationalism nor self-government flourished in Malaya during the Japanese occupation.

Liberation, Union, and Federation. The people of Malaya accepted the return of the British with equanimity, if not with enthusiasm. A British military government restored law and order, but not without charges of corruption, illegal commandeering of property, gunplay against unarmed civilians, and sale of arms to gangsters. The British showed little consideration for an unnerved people. They treated Malaya more like "an Augean stable than the model of smooth administration which it had been."

A British diplomat, Sir Harold MacMichael, induced all the sultans to sign treaties which surrendered sovereignty and constitutional arrangements to the king of England. The sultans were to retain the throne and little else. Laws were no longer to be signed and ratified by the sultans but by a governor-general whose very title symbolized a descent to colonialism. All the Malay states (including the four returned by Thailand) with Penang and Malacca were to be joined into a protectorate—the Malay Union. Common citizenship was to be granted to the Chinese, who still wanted to have Singapore in the Union and more political opportunities for themselves. In protest against the Union, the United Malay National Organization (UMNO) went into mourning for one week over the threatened extinction of their race.

Malcolm MacDonald arrived in Malaya in May, 1946, as the new governor-general. He saw the handwriting on the wall for the Union proposals and presided over their interment. In February, 1948, the Federation of Malaya came into being by joint action of King George and nine sultans. New agreements returned sovereignty to the sultans, who were to rule their states with British advice.

The Federation was to be governed by a High Commissioner, with Executive and Legislative Councils. The High Commissioner was charged with safeguarding the rights of Malayans and maintaining the honor and dignity of the sultans. As further protection for the Malayans, qualifications for citizenship for Chinese were stiffened up. Singapore was not included in the Federation. It was continued as a separate crown colony with its own governor.

The Federation, 1948-1957. Political agitation subsided with the establishment of the Federation. The British rebuilt the civil service and set in motion an excellent program for social welfare. The interests of peasants and workers were taken care of, including the health and education of their children. The national economy was put on a sound basis. Half the rice requirements had to be imported, but foreign exchange was easy, thanks to rubber and tin. A development program—which represented a practical compromise between government planning and private enterprise—called for a balanced growth in agricultural production, industrialization, and expansion in education and the social services. Exporters had their problems because of their dependence upon two major products. Rubber and tin represented one-quarter of the gross national product and from 80 to 85 per cent of the export trade. Moreover, the income which they earned was in dollars. The fluctuating demands of American buyers determined whether it was boom times or hard times in Malaya. There would have been continuous prosperity had it not been for the costs of fighting the terrorists in the jungles.

The Emergency. After 1948, the Communists shifted their major operations from strikes and riots in Singapore to terrorism in Malaya. They were anti-capitalist and anti-foreign. They killed and kidnapped rich Chinese and prosperous British planters. The hard core of the MPAJA became the Malayan Races Liberation Army, with five or six thousand men. As some were killed, they were replaced by new recruits. Inspiration and aid came from China; food and local supplies from the "min yuen," or helpful Chinese villagers. They ambushed travellers, wrecked trains, and destroyed rubber trees. They cost Malaya one-fourth of the national income for pacification. It took the regular army, the air force, the home guards, and the volunteers to beat the terrorists. It also required a vast resettlement program for Chinese squatters, in addition to military measures. By December, 1955, the government (but not the military) felt that the back of the terror was broken and that the fight against the Communists had become a mere annoyance.

In December, 1955, the leader of the Communists—the same Chin Peng who had marched in London—sought a truce with the government. He met with officials in a school house in Baling, Kedah, and offered to surrender. He suggested that his new program of national unity and peace would entitle him to pardon and recognition as a legal political operator. After the breakdown of negotiations, the government permitted the man who cost so much in blood and treasure to return to his jungle hideout.

Merdeka, or Independence. While the British fought the terrorists, they felt obliged to accede to growing demands for self-government. These demands came from a sophisticated elite, not from the fishermen and the farmers. Demands were tardy in appearing because of the jealousies between the racial communities. But when the Malay, Chinese, and Indian communities pooled their talents and concentrated their energies on the colonial system, the British could only retreat as gracefully as possible. They granted more unofficial representation in the councils and inaugurated a modified cabinet system. They authorized elections on the local, and then on the national, level. In the elections of 1955, the Malay-Chinese-Indian (MCI) alliance party won 51 of 52 seats contested for in the legislature and polled 84 per cent of the votes.

The subsequent progress towards Merdeka was not a record of bloodshed and battle, but rather a dignified story of cooperation. When Malaya's first independent legislative council met, it had no member who had been in jail for agitating for self-rule. In February, 1956, the Federation of Malaya Constitutional Conference in London agreed to the transfer of power and suggested the

arget date of August 31, 1957. A joint commission of
distinguished jurists then worked out a constitution which
provided for independence within the commonwealth.
The new state was given the right to choose its own government and to exercise full sovereignty.

The actual process of transferring sovereignty was an
exciting demonstration of successful statecraft. On August 3, 1957, the Sultan of Negri-Sembilan was elected
as Yang-di-Pertuan, or Paramount Ruler. (He was third
in line, but the senior sultan of Johore preferred to remain in London, and the sultan of Pahang ruled himself
out of the running because of the commoner status of his
sultana.) On August 5, the Paramount Ruler and the
High Commissioner signed the agreement to end British
power and jurisdiction. On August 31 the Duke of
Gloucester, representing the queen, formally transferred
power to British-educated Tengku Abdul Rahman, the
chief minister of Malaya, who read the declaration of
independence of Malaya to the crowd assembled in Kuala
Lumpur for the festivities. (*See Reading No. 13.*) At
midnight the lights in the stadium went out (eight minutes
late) and then came on again to signify the beginning of
the new regime. There were shouts of Merdeka, the roll
of drums and the singing of the national anthem. The
new flag was unfurled, and the 101-gun salute was fired.
Finally, the Bilal made the call for Moslem prayer.

Government in Action. With independence, the
Malayans had to meet and solve for themselves the
problems of government. They had to maintain the high
level of the civil service in the face of voluntary retire-
ment of many experienced administrators. They had to
carry forward the economic and social program which
they had inherited. They were challenged to continue
their tradition of civil liberties and individual rights.

The chances were that the feeling between the races
would grow worse. The MCI alliance needed to be reassessed and reorganized. It had served for the allocation
of power pending self-government, but it was an unknown
quantity for the inculcation of a new sense of Malayan
nationality. The Malayans retained privileges in civil service positions, eligibility for scholarships, permits and
licenses for trade, and reservations of land. The Malayan

language was the official language of the state, in spite of Chinese pressure for a multilingual legislature. The Chinese wanted equal rights for all citizens and more liberal citizenship laws. Forty per cent of the Chinese were still excluded from citizenship, and 90 per cent were denied the right to vote.

The Chinese protested against the national education system, which provided for six years of free primary education. The Chinese were jealous of the fate of their own schools. The government had no complaint against legitimate education for the preservation of Chinese culture, but it feared the use by Communists of Chinese schools for subversive purposes. In an effort to weed out agitators, the government ordered the dismissal of over-age students. In cities throughout Malaya, the Chinese students rioted and staged sit-down strikes. The police used tear gas. Then the government closed the schools, arrested and deported the obvious trouble-makers.

The Chinese were also out of sympathy with the government's security program. They would not join the army, and they insisted that money spent on subduing the terrorists should be used for economic development. With regard to emergency regulations, the new government agreed to continue the previous measures for one year. Arrangements were made with the United Kingdom, Australia, and New Zeland to continue their help against the terrorists. The prime minister believed that he could come to terms with Chin Peng during that time. After Merdeka, the government dropped two million leaflets on the Communist strongholds inviting surrender. Communists were given the option of peaceful existence as Malayans or a free trip to Peking. The government wanted peace, but it was unwilling to legalize the Communist Party and Communist organizations.

The new government approached foreign relations with caution. On October 12, 1957, an agreement on external defense and mutual assistance was signed with Great Britain. The British agreed to train and develop the armed forces of Malaya as might be required for external defense; Malaya agreed to make its bases and facilities available for British use. The two governments agreed to consult together and to cooperate in the event of an armed attack or threat to the preservation of peace. Malaya was not very friendly either to Formosa China or mainland China, but it indicated willingness to co-operate with everybody but Peking. It was not disposed to participate in SEATO or any military bloc. On September 17, 1957, it was admitted as the eighty-second member of the United Nations.

Relations with Singapore. The merger of Malaya and Singapore seemed inevitable in due course, but there was no prospect for immediate action. The crux of the issue lay in the following figures:

Population

(1951)	Malays	Chinese	Indians	Others	Total
Singapore	127,063	806,690	75,001	32,579	1,041,933
Federation	2,631,154	2,043,971	586,371	75,726	5,337,222
Total	2,758,217	2,805,661	661,672	108,305	6,379,155

Merger would have meant the extinction of the majority position of the Malays in the Federation; and the consequent extension of the power of the Chinese of Singapore.

Singapore: Communism, and Self-Government. The Chinese of Singapore were themselves vital targets of Nationalist and Communist movements. They were tossed between conflicting pulls of loyalty towards the country of their origin and the country of their domicile. They were repelled or attracted by the tactics of the Communists, depending upon their individual circumstances. They were interested primarily in work and profit, but they could not avoid the compulsions of politics. Many of the successful Chinese would have preferred the security of a continued British regime, but they rose gradually to assume the responsibilities which came with self-government.

According to a Singapore White Paper of August, 1957, the Communists reapplied pressure to the colony after their defeat in the federation. They infiltrated the schools, the trade-unions, and political parties. In 1955 and again the following year, riots in Chinese private schools tested the police powers of the colonial government. They led to the closure of the schools, the dissolution of certain middle-school student unions, and the arrest and expulsion of the ringleaders. The authorities were on constant alert for reappearance of trouble, and they facilitated the move towards independence and statehood as one of the most effective ways to remove a chronic source of irritation.

Singapore's valued strategic position and its role as the chief dollar-earner of the Commonwealth caused the British to look carefully before each forward step. In 1946 Singapore was first set up as a separate colony with its own governor, executive and legislative council. In 1953 the administration was democratized further, but independence was withheld because of the Communist danger. Parties were organized, and in 1955 elections were held. A government was formed by David Marshall, the leader of the Labor Front, in coalition with the Alliance Party composed of the UMNO, the Malay Chinese Association (MCA), and the Singapore-Malay Union. The opposition was formed by the Liberal-Socialists, the Peoples Action Party, and the Independents. Marshall resigned when he failed to get his way with his proposals for more self-government.

A highly respected Chinese, Lim Yew-Hock, followed Marshall. In March, 1957, he conducted successful negotiations with the British for a new state of Singapore. The constitution which was agreed upon recognized full self-government internally for Singapore and left the responsibility for external affairs, defense, and the ultimate right to suspend the constitution in the hands of Her Majesty's government. Singapore was to be ruled by a titular head of state, a prime minister, and a cabinet responsible to a fully elected fifty-one member legislature. The basis of citizenship was broadened and the right to vote extended. It was to be "the deliberate and conscious policy of government to recognize the special position of the Malays, who are the indigenous people of the island and most in need of assistance." The wheels of the machinery for the new government were to be set in motion sometime after January 1, 1958. Singapore was in sight of its immediate goal of self-governing statehood.

THAILAND (SIAM)

A railroad passes from Singapore across Malaya and he Isthmus of Kra to Bangkok, the capital of Thailand. The land frontiers of Thailand are shared with Malaya on the south, with Indochina on the north and east, and with Burma on the north and west. In Southeast Asia, Thailand has two great distinctions: it was never anybody's colony and during World War II it was on the side of Japan.

Riding the Storm with Japan. In December, 1941, when the menacing Japanese armies appeared at Thailand's border and demanded the right of passage, Prime Minister Phibun decided to ride with the storm. The decision was made in the name of the king, and with the assent of the small cabal of politicians—the promoters—which had been the ruling clique since the revolution of 1932. The first fruits of cooperation with Japan were very pleasant. Thailand received coveted territories from Indochina, Malaya, and the Shan states of Burma. It was spared from enemy invasion. Thailand allied itself formally with Japan and in January, 1942, declared war against Britain and the United States. The Siamese did not have to fight. They were called upon for camp sites and barracks, food, supplies, labor, and camp followers. Their sovereignty received a certain outward show of respect from the Japanese, who carried on their operations behind the scenes.

As the war dragged on, the fate of the Thais grew more ominous. Their country was under martial law. Goods became scarcer and more expensive. Trade dwindled away. Chinese investments were wiped out as Japanese *zaibatsu,* or large commercial and financial firms, dominated the Thai market. The dutiful Thai prime minister made appropriate speeches for the Japa-

nese and issued a series of decrees which regulated everything from conduct in the barbershop to clothing the
contented, naked babies.

When the Thais detected the shift in the fortunes of
war, they trimmed their sails. They gave added attention
to the "Free Thai" government, which had been sponsored by their own ambassadors in Washington and London. They volunteered in greater numbers for the resistance movement led by Pridi, the regent of the youthful
king. Foreign paratroopers landing on Thai soil and increasing frequency of American bombing raids made
the Thais eager for uprising.

At the war's end, the Thais were quick to do penance
for their mistakes and win their way back into the good
graces of the victors. They ousted the prime minister,
Phibun, and detained him politely under arrest. The
ruling clique used Pridi to negotiate peace. Thailand was
obliged to expel the Japanese, give up its newly acquired
territories, make its rice surplus available for distribution
elsewhere in Southeast Asia, restore prewar foreign economic rights, and renew its promises regarding a possible
Kra canal. The Thais came to terms with the Kuomintang
government of China, promised most-favored-nation
treatment to the United States, and, in an understanding
with Russia, agreed to legalize the Communist party
within Thailand. Thailand was the first ex-enemy to be
admitted to the United Nations.

Stability and Prosperity.   Thailand's social stability
and economic prosperity made it able to weather political
and diplomatic storms. Thai institutions—the family, the
village, the social hierarchy, and the monarchy—had not
been buffeted about by foreign administrators nor dis-
lodged by alien ideas. In spite of poverty in the hills of
the northwest and on the plateau of the northeast, the
Thais of the river valleys lived well under their own
system of government. They felt no compulsions for a
mysterious something which the west called democracy.
Similarly they had no predilection for communism—
native style, Russian, Chinese, or Vietnamese. They were
prosperous, orderly, and proud of their own land and
their religion. If they were deprived of civil rights, they
were not particularly aware of it. Distant lands with

either the charm of a propagandized socialist paradise or unsurpassed way of life had little appeal for Thais, whose existence was identified with a city, a fishing village, a forest clearing, or a plot of rice-land. Their spiritual needs were filled by Buddhism. Their religion did not depend on coercion or demonstration. It was not a Sunday affair but an essential part of their everyday lives. In their relations with one another, the Thais were dignified and easygoing. Their social safety valves were unrestrained and frequent celebrations.

The ordinary Thai farmers were interested in a high price for rice. For the most part, they were landowners and had little need for reform legislation. They stood to gain from improved irrigation and transportation facilities. They looked to the government for protection against the Chinese buyers, millers, and distributors of rice and for financial help which could keep them out of the clutches of Chinese usurers. On the other hand, the Thai political elite was infected by the virus of riches. It wanted a share of the profits earned by Chinese and Westerners. To this end it adopted a philosophy of national socialism and used the state as its instrument. It devoted little real energy to agricultural problems. It was much more intrigued by industrialization. It argued that the state should take the lead in stimulating trade and building factories. It was aware of the potential personal gain in every contract. Economic development was slow and costly, in spite of nominally strict import and exchange controls. Nonessential goods tended to disappear from the market, and they commanded outrageous prices. Still, spending was conspicuous, and scandals were commonplace. Someone paid for the Cadillacs in Bangkok.

The Chinese. The Thais turned against the Chinese as the major cause of their economic ills. Immediately after World War II—in the general atmosphere of contrition—the Thais eased upon the Chinese and received a swarm of Chinese immigrants. In 1948, while the Kuomintang was in power in China, the Thais adopted new measures of repression. They reduced the annual immigration quota from ten thousand to two hundred. They restricted the Chinese embassy in its functions and closed the Chinese consulates. They exercised careful control over the Chinese schools and Chinese newspapers

The Thais were worried by the Communist victory ir China and by the Chinese advance in Korea. They tightened the naturalization laws and assessed a high registration fee for aliens. In 1952 they passed a severe anti-subversives act which outlawed the Communist Party As international tensions eased, the Thais shifted their policies from the iron fist to the velvet glove. They offered assimilation as a way to escape discrimination They halved the registration fee and liberalized election laws. They granted more privileges to persons of Chinese descent in matters of land ownership and military service They opened Thai labor unions for Chinese membership

The Thais and the Chinese avoided serious troubles because they both exhibited consummate skill in the subtleties of compromise. The Thais and the Chinese were useful to each other. The political elite was Thai ir citizenship, but partially Chinese in its blood. It had prestige, but it needed rich relatives, Chinese or other wise, to pay the bills. It was, to a Chinese, an advantage to have a son or daughter married to a highly placed Thai or his relative. There was a constant pay-off be tween Thai politicians and Chinese merchants. Further down the scale there was a standard operating procedure of squeeze and bribery. Many shops displayed the limited partnership sign—which indicated a nominal Thai owner ship but with Chinese relatives or brains behind the business.

The Art of the Coup d'État. The king and the common people were relatively untouched by constant shifts in political power. Government turnovers mean little more than regroupment of personnel and reappor tionment of the spoils among the four thousand or so who constituted the elite. In the three years after 1945 nine governments came and went before Phibun—the ex-collaborator with the Japanese—re-established himsel in authority. He sent his chief rival, Pridi, into exile to China because of complicity in the death of the king— death which the jury conservatively ruled was "either accident, suicide, or murder." Phibun survived one at tempted coup d'état after another. Once he escaped death because he was a good swimmer; again because o

convenient stomach pump; and a third time because
is assailant was an incredibly bad shot. His policy was
) please Great Britain and the United States. His star
)se to the zenith with the appearance of the Communist
nenace. Whatever else he had been, or was, became im-
naterial. He was regarded as the strongest anti-Commu-
ist in Southeast Asia.

During his ten years as prime minister, from 1948 to
957, political power gravitated towards three men—
hibun himself, Phao Sriyanond, the chief of police, and
arit Thanarat, field marshal of the 85,000-man army.
ach tried to outjockey the other. In February, 1957,
hibun ordered an election. He felt that a victory at the
olls would strengthen his hand and demonstrate his
opularity. Phibun's party captured the National As-
embly—which was half-nominated, half-elected—but it
on because of stuffing the ballot box, intimidating the
oters and manipulating returns. Phao's police cooperated
the irregularities. Sarit dared to comment that the
ection was completely illegal on all sides. Students at
hulalongkorn University, in a gesture of protest, flew
ie flag at half-mast for "our dead democracy." Phibun's
chemes backfired. He lost public acclaim, while Sarit
iined it. Then Phibun ordered all military commanders
nd cabinet officers to sever their commercial connec-
ons. Sarit balked because of his interest in tens of com-
anies and his headship of the lucrative government
ttery. Sarit gradually withdrew from the Phibun regime.
e felt that Phibun and Phao were out to get him and
self-defense he had better take action quickly.

On September 16, 1957, after informing the king of
s plans, Sarit moved. Without bloodshed, without firing
shot, he took over police headquarters, bridges, high-
ays, and vital communications centers. The only hitch
ccurred in police headquarters where an American diplo-
atic officer was so unlucky as to be caught and nearly
iot while valuable papers were being burned. The peo-
e clanging to work on noisy street cars were not aware
iat anything had happened. Then Sarit published his
iarges against Phibun's government (of which he him-
elf had been one of the strongest members). He said the
overnment was unable to keep order, was guilty of in-

efficient financial administration, followed an inept for
eign policy, provided insufficient education for the people
permitted high prices and low living standards, pursue
a poor economic policy, promoted corrupt practice
harbored cabinet officers who did not keep their promise
(chiefly Phao's father-in-law, the Minister of Industries)
and in general conducted an irresponsible, antidemo
cratic administration.

Phibun and Phao were ousted. Phibun shipped some o
his possessions to Cambodia and left for Japan. Sarit sai
Phibun could come back and live wherever and howeve
he pleased. This led some to suspect that Sarit and Phibu
had staged a joint plot to get rid of Phao. Phao enplane
for Switzerland (where his money was) and said "Every
thing is fine. I am going abroad for two or three year
There will be no trouble as Sarit is my friend." But Sarit
papers called Phao the man who had turned Thailan
into a kingdom of fear and described how Phao ha
made millions out of opium.

Sarit had no precise political program, as his mai
interests were economic. He was no more "democratic
or concerned about civil rights than his predecessor. H
was expected to rearrange, but not to abolish, the evi
of which he himself had complained. He dissolved th
old assembly. He named his henchmen as the appointe
half of a new assembly, which chose unanimously Po
Sarassin—a man who had served five years as the Th
ambassador in Washington and loved every minute o
it—as prime minister. Sarit was made commander i
chief of the navy and the air force as well as the arm
and the overthrow of Phibun was made legal. An electic
for the remaining half of the assembly was set up fo
December, 1957, so that the people "might have a ne
government as a New Year's present."

The election was a concession to mollify the swellin
rumbles against corruption. Daily scandals in the Ban,
kok press prompted readers to ask about graft whic
was undiscovered or hushed up. As public educatic
spread, so did public enlightenment. Students voiced th
general disgust, at the risk of being branded as Comm
nists by the party in power. The election was a tran
parent sop. The government's majority in the assembl

was assured by the appointed members, and government supporters were certain to win at the polls. A multitude of candidates campaigned in a halfhearted way. Phibun's party practically disappeared, and Independents stood on platitudes. The platform of the Democrats was anti-corruption and anti-communism. A Socialist Front rallied around very strong leftist policies: collective farms, opposition to imperialist America, abolition of SEATO, and repeal of the anti-subversives act. Only 20 per cent of the apathetic voters went to the polls, and their votes continued the old order intact. The ailing Marshal Sarit, and the simmering clique around him, wielded the power behind the throne with his National Socialist Party.

Skilful Diplomacy. Thai's internal political moves were not without diplomatic significance. Until the coup d'état of September, 1957, Thailand was taken for granted in the American camp. Phibun was looked upon as a puppet of the United States. From 1950-1956 he received $112,000,000 from America in nonmilitary aid and unspecified millions more in military assistance. His departure coincided with a rising tide of criticism of the United States. Typical sentiments were, "We are loyal Thais, not loyal Americans," "We have too many loudmouthed American advisers," and "How can we prepare against the bandits who are already in our house?" The United States seemed to lose, and China to gain, in prestige.

The replacement of Phibun by Sarit did not indicate an abrupt change in attitude, but it presaged the classic Thai diplomatic game of hedging. Sarit was very friendly to American officers, and he profited from American aid. Although ostensibly pro-American in policy, he was not without alternatives in his dealings with the United States. He had to be extremely careful toward China because of his own minority group and the geographic nearness of the Chinese state. The Laos corridor led directly to Thailand from China. He wanted to be prepared in the event the United States should reduce its commitments in Thailand or recognize Red China. He relaxed the trade ban on nonstrategic goods and cautiously permitted the exchange of some persons. He also made new estimates of the advantages of neutralism. He could not fail to notice the growing American tolerance of neutralism and the ability of the neutrals to attract aid from both sides of the Iron Curtain.

In addition to American sources, Thailand received aid from the World Bank and from nations in the Colombo Plan. It also looked hopefully for new help from Japan. It was the Asian headquarters for many agencies of the United Nations, and its distinguished representative, Prince Wan Wathaiyakorn, served as president of the General Assembly. Among its neighbors, Thailand favored South Vietnam more than the north, and it maintained a lively interest in the affairs of the Buddhist bloc of Cambodia, Laos, and Burma. Its contemporary diplomats measured up to the traditionally high Thai standards of skill and adroitness.

— 7 —

BURMA

Thailand's neighbor to the west and north, which has been through the years more an enemy than a friend, is Burma. The Burmans, since independence, have been less concerned about the Thais, whom they think they can handle, than about their other neighbors, the Indians and the Chinese. The full name of Burma is the Republic of the Union of Burma, and the key word is *Union*. Almost half the state is made up of minority groups. The Indians and the Chinese are scattered throughout the country. In contrast, the Shans, Kachins, Chins, Arakanese, and Karens are concentrated in distinct regions— almost separate worlds—with marked degrees of autonomy. Those people are *Burman*, in that they live in Burma, but they are different from the majority *Burmese*

acial group, which lives and rules in and around Rangoon. The fundamental problem of Burma—as of Indonesia—is the preservation of the territorial integrity of the
state.

Under the Japanese. When World War II threatened, some Burmese leaders including Ba Maw and
Thakin Nu were in jail; Aung San and his thirty comrades were in Formosa; and U Saw, the prime minister,
was in England negotiating for more independence. Burmans welcomed the Japanese at first, but their enthusiasm
quickly cooled. (*See Reading No. 17.*) "We hoped that
we would get independence, but all we got was slapped
faces, ruined homes, looted property, and forced labor."
Ba Maw, with Thakin Nu and others, formed a puppet
government, which was granted independence in 1943;
Aung San and his brother-in-law, Than Thun, organized
the Burma Independence Army, which the Japanese renamed the Burma Defense Army; and the most Com-
munistic of the Burmese nationalists—foreseeing that
they had more to fear ultimately from the Japanese than
the British—printed anti-Japanese leaflets and established
contacts with the British in India. The reconquest of
Burma was the largest single land campaign against the
Japanese. In August, 1944, Aung San and his companions
organized the Anti-Fascist Peoples Freedom League
(AFPFL) made up of Socialists, Communists, and non-
descripts, whose only common denominator was anti-
Japan. As the end of the war approached, Aung San
transferred his resistance army openly to the side of the
Allies.

Independence. After the Japanese surrender, the
British were prepared to make concessions to Burma in
the direction of self-government. But not enough to satisfy
the Burmans. Dominion status offered too little to Nationalists, who dropped the title of Thakin for U, or
uncle, which is given to every Burmese of standing. The
threat of anarchy made it imperative to come to terms
with the British. Aung San, the elected head of the
government, conducted negotiations in spite of Communist objections. He expelled the Communists from the
AFPFL rather than give in to their pressure. As a penalty
for his firmness, he and six of his colleagues on the way

out of a cabinet meeting were machine-gunned in col
blood by assassins hired by U Saw. (U Saw was execute
for his part in the crime.) Thakin Nu—or U Nu—as
sumed the responsibilities of prime minister which h
exercised for many years. On October 17, 1947, he cor
cluded a treaty of independence with the sympatheti
Labor Government. In accordance with this agreemen
a financial settlement was reached; a British naval, ai
and military mission was to be accepted in Burma; an
Burma's ports and airfields were to be accessible to Britis
forces. In January, 1948, Burma declared its complet
independence from Great Britain and was admitted t
the United Nations.

Civil War and Banditry. Chaos followed independ
ence. Law and order disappeared with the removal c
British prestige, economic power, and the British army
The inherently unstable social order collapsed. Burmes
and minority groups went after each other like fightin
cocks. The governing elite—which was smaller an
younger in Burma than in other countries of Southea
Asia—splintered into irreconcilable factions. The Con
munists divided into Stalinist and Trotskyite parties an
separately resumed civil war. Part of the former freedor
fighters, the Peoples Volunteer Organization (PVO
rebelled. To cap the climax, the Karen National Defens
Organization, with some of the best soldiers in Burm
took up arms against the government. The countrysic
was unsafe and travel impossible. Only four or five citie
including Rangoon, were secure.

U Nu built up his army and created the Union Militar
Police. He activated village defense forces of uneve
quality. He soon discovered that fighting bandits was lil
chasing a will o' the wisp. He took a firm stand again
the insurgents. He refused to listen to "demands," b
he promised good treatment to all who would surrende

He proceeded on the assumption that pacification cou
not be achieved by arms alone but would have to l
followed inevitably by social improvement. He began l
sponsoring religious revival among the Buddhists. H
established the Bureau of Special Investigation (BSI)
weed out graft and corruption in government. He sa
he did not want Burma to go the way of Kuomintar

China. He advocated educational improvement, better public health, and cheaper housing. He set up the Burma Translation Society for foreign books. He popularized the slogan "Love Burma, Speak Burmese, Encourage Burmese literature." In a burst of enthusiasm for adult education, he said (while the outlaws were at the northern gates of Rangoon), "Many branches of foreign knowledge such as the quantum theory, relativity, geopolitics, and the theory of surplus value will now be within easy reach of our cowherds, cultivators, hewers of wood, and drawers of water."

He endeavored to apply his doctrinaire socialism to the removal of economic abuses and social injustices. His programs for redistribution of land, better tenancy conditions and easier credit, reclamation and irrigation, and amelioration or elimination of debts, were effective pacifiers. He made the rebel leaders "objects of scorn and ridicule, running to keep out of reach of the very people to whom they promised a heaven on earth." By 1951 he felt that he had made sufficient progress to risk a general election. Highways and rivers were not completely safe, and villages were not free from payments of protection money. Ministers in Rangoon lived behind armed guards, but the integrity of the state was no longer in question.

Ideology, Government, and Politics. Ideology was not for the masses, but only for the political elite. Its ideology was a combination of Buddhism, and escape from the world, and socialism, a desire to improve the world. Burmese socialism consisted of prewar Marxism plus a devotion to the welfare state adopted from the British Labor Party. Burmese leaders did not consider socialism as disguised communism or as a step toward communism. They rejected any marriage of convenience with the Communists. They committed themselves to the defense of democracy and rejected Communist amoralism on the issue of means and ends. They opposed old and new colonialism. U Kyaw Nyein said, "To my mind both types of colonialism are dangerous. In fact the Soviet type of imperialism is perhaps even more degrading and dangerous, because it is more ruthless, more systematic, and more blatantly justified in the name of the world Communist revolution."

The Constitution of 1947 reflected the philosophy of socialism. It gave to the state the right to limit foreign property and to expropriate by law. It permitted nationalization of natural resources, water transport, rice export, and national financial institutions. The constitution modelled the government after the British pattern. The legislature consisted of a Chamber of Nationalities (63 Burmese and 62 of other races) and a Chamber of Deputies of 250 delegates. The executive consisted of a titular president, the prime minister, and three deputy prime ministers. The judiciary was independent.

The government was democratic in form and in name, but it was a one-party, one-man-controlled oligarchy in practice. The Socialist Party dominated the AFPFL, and U Nu directed the party. The charmed circle of the AFPFL, with its monopoly of talent and its connections with peasants and workers, ran the government much as it pleased. It commanded the army and kept officials in line through the BSI. A handful of men distributed jobs, made decisions, and did the administrative work. Only the western-trained junior executives, who were confident of their own abilities, dared openly to express dissatisfaction. Sub-surface dissension plagued the AFPFL.

The national election of 1956 for a five-year term in the Chamber of Deputies was not a contest of ideologies. It was scarcely a test of strength against the well-entrenched AFPFL. The AFPFL got 48 per cent of the votes and 170 seats; the opposition National Unity Front (NUF) got 30 per cent of the votes but only 50 seats. Since the Communists were outlawed as a party in 1953, the extremists worked through a Burma Workers and Peasants party, which formed the heart of the NUF. They had some able spokesmen, but they had little ammunition against the leftist program of the AFPFL. The NUF, by its impressive showing against handicaps at the polls, served notice that it would be a significant factor in elections ahead.

Pyidawtha, or the Happy Land.   In Burma, politics and economics were inseparable. The AFPFL managed to take advantage of Burma's fundamental economic soundness and win popular support for the well-publicized four-year plans to convert Burma into a *Pyidawtha*. They referred a word meaning happy to one meaning prosperous.

When the government faced the tasks of rehabilitation fter World War II, its greatest asset was Burma's natural wealth. Rice existed in abundance on the farms and in the villages for Burma's comparatively scant population. Optimism about Burma's economic future increased with istance from Rangoon. Because of the absence of a ense of urgency, the government invited British and American firms to undertake extensive surveys of fundamental needs and to make recommendations for long-term reconstruction.

The stark fact emerged that in spite of national wealth, the Burman level of living was 30 per cent below prewar, when it was about 1/100 that of the United States. Less than one-half the arable land was under cultivation, and productivity was low. The rice trade was in the doldrums. Burman capital was not forthcoming for revival of industries, mines, or transport. Burmans had no money for investment, but plenty for pagodas or *pwe*, the vaudeville celebrations which honored auspicious occasions like a son's entering the monastery or the piercing f a daughter's ears.

The first four-year plan for *Pyidawtha* announced goals to be achieved by 1956. It was not a carefully conceived, well-rounded plan for economic development, but it was n imprecise blueprint for everybody's happiness through industrial expansion and improved social services. It was to be achieved by cooperation at all levels—local, state, and national. The government took the initiative. It retained the services of as many as three hundred foreign technicians and invited foreign capital. Its best-laid schemes went awry. Income dropped because of a slump n rice. Civil wars and disorder, lack of capital and trained personnel thwarted the hoped-for development. n 1956 Burma had just about regained its prewar economic level, which was by then only 1/500 the current level in the United States. Burma's experience illustrated the widening gap between western and more recently developed countries.

An article in *The Guardian,* Rangoon, April, 1957, p. described the practical difficulties in Burma's economic development:

"There is general uneasiness at the role of government in business. One aspect of failure is as old as Asia—squeeze all along the line. The ideas are fine—the more government control, the more benefit to the masses. The middleman and his profit are discredited beyond redemption. The government will preside between the sources of supply and the ultimate consumer. (Hence that monstrous incubus, the Civil Supplies Organization with an establishment that would cripple a private firm; hence the Purchasing Mission that so blithely bartered away advantages and opportunities.) In practice it is not the consumer who benefits. He must pay an invisible margin of tea money and squeeze. Red tape means incalculable loss of man hours. Papers must be signed in triplicate, scrutinized. Waiting for people to appear; to get on with their job when they do appear and undo mistakes they should never have made; waiting for endless checks and counter checks—waiting made all the more galling by the knowledge that a bit of judicious palm-greasing would escape it all. . . .

Is there not something repugnant in the idea of a citizen having to stand cap in hand for commodities and service he must pay for in any case? The time has come to weed out graft if it is not to strangle progress and make nonsense of fine schemes for serving the public welfare."

The second four-year plan was announced in 1957. It reversed the order of priorities by placing law and order before economic development and social services. It offered even greater attractions for foreign capital. It did not abandon faith in the principles of socialism. It recognized the prevalence of self-interest and attempted to canalize self-interest into public service. It estimated that Burma would need a billion American dollars—three quarters from foreign sources—in ten years to increase by 10 per cent the per capita rate of consumption.

Foreign Aid. When Burma thought of foreign loans, it turned again to the United States. From 1950 to 1953 it had accepted American aid, with strings, and in 1954 it announced that it would be interested in loans without political implications. In 1957 it concluded satisfactory arrangements for a new American loan of $42,

000,000. It obtained other loans from India, the World Bank, and the Monetary Fund. It received help from the private agencies of the United Nations and from the "giver" nations of the Colombo plan. Trucks on the streets of Rangoon with "Japanese Reparations" painted on the side symbolized the $25,000,000 per year which Burma was to receive for ten years from Japan. From the Soviet bloc, Burma obtained goods and services to pay for a third of its rice crop, which it bartered away.

Successful Neutralism. Half of Burma's foreign policy was the disposal of its rice crop; the other half was making neutralism work. (*See Reading No. 18.*) Burma was the most successful of the neutrals in standing for peace and getting the best of both worlds for itself. It was an active Colombo power and a leader in Asian conferences, but it refused to join in military blocs. It revoked its pact with Great Britain in 1953 and declined membership in SEATO. It insisted on the elimination of every condition of mutual security before renewing its loan negotiations with the United States. It took a firm stand against Li Mi and the Kuomintang guerrillas when they established themselves in the mountainous frontier between Burma and China.

Burma later disputed a frontier zone, through which a vital highway passed, with Communist China. Burmese public opinion was in no mood to accept surrender of any territory under pressure. The government was inclined to admit some reason in the Chinese position. When boundary adjustments had been made in 1897 and 1941, the British in Burma had derived advantage from the hopelessness of the Chinese diplomatic arguments. So far as the mountain people in the disputed area were concerned, "5 per cent were for Burma, 5 per cent were for China and 90 per cent were indifferent to everything except their flocks or their caravans." Burma was among the first to recognize and to exchange ambassadors with Red China. Rangoon and Peking were linked by direct air service, and in 1957 almost 2,500 Burmese visited mainland China. Burma sold substantial quantities of rice to China, including that which was bartered by China to Ceylon for rubber.

U Nu's personal relations with foreign peoples and

powers were fortuitous. He was well received in Washington, Moscow, and Peking. He graciously entertained Khrushchev and Bulganin; Tito; Chou En-lai; and Lord Mountbatten and Sir Hubert Rance, the last British governor of Burma. But with all his foreign contacts, he warned his own people, "Beware of pied pipers who are chanting new tunes that open up entrancing visions of imaginary wonderlands. These tunes find their way into Burma where men and women who are deluded by them stir up ruinous trouble. They are like foolish children who listen to their distant aunt rather than their own mother."

— 8 —

VIETNAM, CAMBODIA, AND LAOS: THE FORMER INDOCHINA

During World War II. The nationalists of Indochina were found almost exclusively among the Vietnamese, who constituted 75 per cent of the population. Some nationalists welcomed the Japanese attack on the French position. Others, including the Communists, opposed the Japanese as the greater menace to ultimate independence. No resistance was possible to the prewar Japanese advances which converted Indochina into an ideal starting area for the attack on the southern regions.

Throughout the war, France and Japan played a cat-and-mouse game in Indochina. The governor-general under the Pétain regime, Admiral Decoux, collaborated outwardly in order to preserve French sovereignty. The Japanese recognized the French technical position and played down the theme of independence. However, they catered to the Vietnamese and stressed the propaganda of Asia for the Asiatics. Vietnamese nationalists seemed to receive sympathy from the Japanese, nothing but suppression from the French. The underground, such as it was, was inspired by the Viet Minh, or League for the Independence of Vietnam, which was organized in south China. It was not very effective until the last stages of the war when it received substantial American help.

On March 9, 1945, the Japanese became fed up with French vacillation. Admiral Decoux was ousted; French troops and administrative personnel were interned. With Japanese blessing, Bao Dai, the emperor of Annam under the French, was enabled to declare the independence of what was soon to be renamed Vietnam. The kings of Cambodia and Laos were likewise permitted to declare independence. From then on the three states went their separate ways. On the French side, General De Gaulle announced that after the war a quasi-independent Indochina would be a member of the French Union. In July, 1945, at Potsdam, the allies planned for the liberation by the Chinese in the north and by the British in the south, pending the return of the French. But far away from the spotlight and in the hills of Tongking, the Viet Minh organized a provisional government for Vietnam. As quickly as the Japanese toppled, Bao Dai abdicated his uneasy throne and transmitted his powers to the provisional government which moved into Hanoi. In a document more reminiscent of America than Russia, on September 2, 1945, Vietnam declared its independence. (*See Reading No. 19.*)

The French encountered but slight resistance on their return to Cambodia and Laos. With Vietnam it was different. Ho Chi Min was the man of the hour. He sent Bao Dai, ex-emperor turned private citizen, as his adviser on an indeterminate assignment to Hongkong. He overcame his rivals, who were supported by the Chinese Kuomintang, and set up a constitutional structure within which he could carry out his ideas. He expressed his program in words of one syllable which appealed to the peasants. He advocated less taxes, lower rents, and no forced labor; he promised more food, better health, and better schools. The subtleties of ideology were left to the intellectuals. In November, 1945, he replaced the Communist party with an Association for the Study of Marxism.

On February 28, 1946, Ho and the French came to terms with the Chinese, whereupon the Chinese troops—with a black record of rape and loot—left Vietnam. Within a week, March 6, Ho obtained from the French an agreement by which France would recognize Vietnam as a free (but not independent) state within the French Union. As French troops began to return to the north, Ho went to France to conclude a modus vivendi in September, 1946—which was the last agreement between the Viet Minh and France until 1954.

Outbreak of War. Shortly after Ho's return, war broke out between the Vietnamese and the French. Each side placed the blame upon the other. The fighting was mild at first. Ho said the Vietnamese would cooperate with the French, if the French would do as the Americans had done in the Philippines or the British had done in India. The French were determined by that time, early 1947, to keep Vietnam out of the hands of Ho, who had become, in their opinion, a pawn of Moscow. French unwillingness to make concessions to nationalism was a glaring mistake. Ho and his doctrinaire colleagues captured the leadership of the nationalist revolution. Ho's men were not mere agitators or convicts, they represented the nationalist cause. They shackled it with the pattern of a classical Communist organization.

As the war dragged on, the French tried a new tactic of splitting the Vietnamese. The Communist victory in China gave a new depth to the picture in Indochina. A local war loomed as the next likely spot in a global conflict. The French enticed Bao Dai to head up a rival government. After December 30, 1949, when Bao Dai took over the reins in the south, the word "Vietnam" had two meanings. Ho clung to his use of Vietnam as meaning the Democratic Republic of Vietnam (DRV) in the north; Bao Dai and the French appropriated the word as referring to the new government at Saigon. Bao was no match for Ho as the exponent of Vietnamese nationalism. His white sharkskin suits, fluent French, and clumsy Vietnamese, and corpulent fondness for French cooking contrasted sharply with Ho's wispy frame and plain clothes of black or khaki. The unequal contest had serious international implications. By February, 1950, Ho gained the recognition of the Soviet bloc, but he spurned the overtures of Tito. Bao Dai received the backing of nations represented by France, the United States, and the United Kingdom. In June, 1950, the Korean "police action" broke out, and President Truman immediately stepped up American aid to the Vietnam of Bao Dai and France. American influence in policy grew with the expanding portion of bills paid by the United States.

From 1950 to 1954—from the Communist conquest of China to the Geneva agreements—the character of the civil war in Indochina changed. Ho tightened up his own command. In 1951 he changed his study group into the Lao Dang, or Working Peoples Party, and he established a Lien Viet, or United National Front. He declared his war was an integral part of the world revolution led by Russia. He formulated new military tactics: first win the people, then the supply lines, and then attack the forts. Vo Nguyen Giap—a former history teacher—with aid and assistance transformed the ragged guerrillas into a capable army.

On the other side, Bao Dai entrusted local administration of affairs to the mandarin class of wealthy, French-educated Vietnamese. He left the fighting to the French. In France, between escapades, he negotiated vainly for more independence. While diplomats procrastinated, soldiers died. The northern Vietnamese, henceforward called simply Viet Minh, killed French officers faster than St. Cyr could graduate them. Supplies were exhausted faster than France and the United States could provide them. The bloody path ended at Dien Bien Phu—and the conference tables at Geneva.

The Geneva Agreements. (*See Reading Nos. 20-22.*) The nation-states of Indochina were less interested in the negotiations at Geneva as a world settlement than as milestones in their own future. Hostilities were ended. Peace brought recognition of their sovereignty, independence, unity, and territorial integrity. But Vietnam was partitioned after the manner of Germany and Korea, and actual unity was left for elections fixed for the summer of 1956. France accepted these arrangements, so did the Viet Minh. But South Vietnam felt that it had no voice in its own fate, and withheld its signature.

The terms of peace for Cambodia provided for the withdrawal of foreign troops and for the incorporation of the Khmer rebels into the national army. Cambodia agreed to undertake no military alliances, give no military bases, and receive no military assistance except in actual defense of the country. Laos fared equally well. Troops were withdrawn, and Laos was prohibited from receiving all types of armaments except as necessary for the defense of Laos. Laos also agreed not to join military alliances so long as its security was not threatened. Laos permitted the French to continue their military mission and retain their bases at Xien Khouang and Seno. Rebel troops of the Pathet Lao, or Country of Lao, were to be assembled into two provinces in the northeast—Phong Saly and Sam Neua—pending final understandings between the leader of the rebels and the royal government.

The Democratic Republic of Vietnam. The DRV came away from Geneva with a feeling of victory, but it too was glad for the return of peace. It suffered from the civil war and needed to rest, reconstitute the army, and strengthen the party. In 1955, before the twentieth party congress in Moscow, the DRV announced an over-all Fatherland Front for all its people. Its policies were mild towards everyone except the "American imperialists." Its platform promised unification of Vietnam, prosperity, high wages, short working hours, and large profits. Government positions were shifted without affecting the tight control by Ho Chi Min and his close associate.

Politically, the DRV called for implementation of the Geneva agreements. It wanted elections as prescribed, but it insisted upon no interference from the outside and freedom of activities for patriotic parties, groups, and social organizations. This would have provided a field day for subversion in which the south was unwilling to compete. As the south increased its strength, the north swelled its chorus for unification. The DRV refrained from the use of force, perhaps due to the counsel of its backers, who would be called upon for unlimited aid.

Economically, the DRV faced a new set of conditions. It was one thing to blow up buildings and bridges; it was another thing to reconstruct. It also faced the inescapable problems of a low level of living, meager income, and high prices. Starvation threatened when partition cut off the traditional import of rice from the rich Mekong delta. Taxes and rents were still burdensome. The farmers clamored for relief and fundamental changes in agrarian reform. Before Geneva, the DRV concentrated on the elimination of usury; after Geneva, particularly after the exodus of a million refugees, it shifted the emphasis towards integration of tiny farms and collectivization. Lands of French imperialists, traitorous Vietnamese, and despotic landlords were confiscated.

Economic relief by industrialization was a distant mirage, since the DRV had neither the men, nor the means, nor the experience. It would require time to repair roads and railways; to rehabilitate mines and factories; to build new industries and shipping facilities; and to revive the commercial life of Hanoi and Haphong. The regime issued regulations for its own national bank and currency, and for the control of its customs and foreign trade. But its progress and prosperity depended uniquely upon Russia, China, and the satellite bloc.

In foreign policy, the DRV regarded itself as a brother socialist nation and not as a satellite. (*See Reading No. 23*.) It accepted the general policies of Russia and China. It granted national status to the Chinese in north Vietnam and permitted the Chinese Communists to operate their own party apparatus on Vietnamese soil. Ho courted the recognition of neutrals and boasted of his new understanding with Tito. He clamped down upon many French investments in his territory, but he sought to preserve his cultural contacts with France, and with many of the forty thousand Vietnamese in France. He maintained propaganda and procurement offices in tolerant countries of Southeast Asia and expressed his desire to lead liberation movements in Thailand, Burma, Malaya, Cambodia, and Laos.

South Vietnam. After Geneva, South Vietnam faced a dim future. Its guardian, France, had been defeated; its new mentor, the United States, was untested. The political system was bankrupt, the administration disorganized, the economy shattered, and the treasury empty. The country was plagued with politico-religious armed sects, which had carved it up and appropriated its best parts. The army was shapeless and in the hands of foreigners. Nearly one million refugees, a tenth of the population, had to be fed, clothed, housed, and resettled. It seemed impossible to preserve South Vietnam as a viable, independent state against its three enemies: colonialism, feudalism, and communism.

Its success depended upon the ability of a new leader, Ngo Dinh Diem, encouraged and assisted by the United States. Diem established law and order, crushed the main strength of the sects, put his own trusted followers in administrative posts, and rebuilt the army. Although aristocratic and diffident by nature, he sought to win the loyalty of the common people from Uncle Ho.

His basic problems were those of the common people. Their age-old way of life—bounded by the rice fields, the village, and the emperor—had been upset. The dependence of the poor upon the rich had been destroyed. The process of assimilation carried on by the French had been interrupted prematurely. No time had been given for training in individual responsibility and self-government. The last eight years had covered the land with hatred and arson, the misery and murder of civil war. In the west there was talk of democracy in South Vietnam; in South Vietnam there was no basis upon which democracy could be built. Ngo Dinh Diem's fundamental task was to provide work so that in the near future there should be no more filthy shacks or crowded slums, and no more underfed, ragged people.

His economic program called for the completion of economic independence and the renovation of the national economy. He tried to replace foreigners—French, Indians, and primarily the Chinese—by Vietnamese in the national economy. He ended the treaties which accorded economic privileges to the Chinese and decreed assimilation or abandonment of their chief commercial and professional activities. He pushed agrarian reform. He wanted to ease the farmers' financial burdens, to modernize methods of agriculture, to provide means for tenants to become small landowners, to distribute lands more equitably, and to orient large landowners towards industrial undertakings. He ignored theoretic distinctions between socialism and free enterprise. He sponsored laws and projects which would reconcile the interests of the state and the legitimate requirements of foreign investors.

The theories of Ngo Dinh Diem differed from his political practices. In his theory the spiritual basis of political life was all-important: "peoples' dreams are the fountain at which we drink." He believed the sole legitimate end and object of the state was to protect the fundamental rights of the human person to existence and the free development of his intellectual, moral, and spiritual life. Important things were in his estimation either good or evil. Communism was evil—it was atheistic materialism. He knew at first hand its tyranny and its terror. Democracy was good—it was the permanent effort to find the right political means for all citizens to develop their maximum potentialities.

In practice, he asserted that western-type regimes were not in accord with social characteristics of Asian countries or with the present situation in Asia. He believed that it was necessary to consider the over-all situation, to control and to guide it. His guidance consisted of installing himself as premier and then as president. He facilitated the election of a national assembly which passed his own constitution. The constitution of October 26, 1956, delegated unusually strong powers to the executive and guaranteed the rights of a citizen only in the absence of a state of crisis. He outlawed the Communist Party. He rejected all overtures towards unification until he was guaranteed that north Vietnam would place the interests of the country above Communist imperialism.

In foreign policy, President Diem said that Vietnam must be independent, Asian, free, peace-loving, and progressive. His people were bitter in their memories of French policy, but grateful for the culture which they inherited. They appreciated American aid—which paid as high as 85 per cent of their budget commitments—but they needed time to adjust to Americans and their ways. On occasions resentment burst forth in gestures of disapproval or a bombing outrage. In all Southeast Asia, their hatred of Communists was deepest. It was based on suffering and unforgettable memories. But it was not enough to plunge them unreservedly into the camp of the Americans or to blind them to alternative avenues of peace and progress. (*See Reading No. 24.*)

Cambodia. Before Geneva, not even the glories of Angkor Wat inspired ambitions for former greatness. After Geneva, Prince Norodom Sihanouk, the one-time king who resigned in favor of his father, symbolized every aspect of national life. Sometimes he was prime minister, sometimes he was not. He held the destiny of his country in his whimsical palm. He created the Peoples Social Community Party, which could deliver practically a 100 per cent vote for him in the elections or the National Assembly.

Cambodia's real problems were comparatively simple. The country was not overpopulated, nor did it suffer from grinding poverty. It was not too unhappy in the ignorance of its own backwardness. Few people found it easier to make a living than the Cambodians. It was said "Stick a seed into the ground and a plant grows; throw a net into the water and it sags with fish." Satisfaction, disinterest, and lethargy worked against political progress or social change; and the Cambodian countryside seemed to be the incarnation of peace.

In foreign policy, Prince Norodom Sihanouk was the soul of contradiction. His country was the traditional enemy of the Thais, yet it offered asylum to Phibun Songgram, the deposed premier. He was known to toy with the idea of a Buddhist federation which would extend from Laos to Burma. He permitted diplomatic talks with north Vietnam, while he kept the border closed to south Vietnam. His countrymen retained French as their second language, but they erased every political tie with the French union. He accepted aid wherever he could get it: the United Nations, the Colombo Powers, France, Japan, China, Russia, or the United States. While America paid practically all the costs of his 35,000-man army, the Prince opined that he would prefer a Swiss-style national guard with professionals only in the technical services. His economic aid did not blunt the independence of his political observations. He expressed approval of the five principles of Chou En-lai and told Americans "you bring us only refrigerators and motor cars." It was his opinion that "your SEATO offers us protection which can only bring us dishonor." His maxim, which earned for him the title of the most successful neutralist in Southeast Asia was "if you want peace, don't prepare for war; don't talk war; stay away from every preparation that may contribute to war."

Laos. Laos is even more backward than Cambodia. In most regions there is scarcely a consciousness of the existence of a state, let alone a spirit of nationalism. There is little urge for betterment of any kind, and a feudal hierarchy—headed by a king—rules as it has for centuries. A very small elite carries the burden of modernization on its shoulders. Any progress is commendable, regardless of labels. After Geneva, France and the United States engaged in a deadly serious effort to thwart the advance of the Communists, as represented by the Pathet Lao. Military and economic progress depended upon foreign effort, and political power depended upon endless jockeying. The succession to King Sisavong Vang was at stake. The choice might have gone to the popular crown prince, Savang Vatthana, or Prince Boun Oum, the inspector-general of the kingdom, or Prince Petsarath, known locally as the eldest of the three half-brothers, distant nephews of the king. The second half-brother, Prince Souvanna Phouma, was the perennial prime minister, and the third half-brother, Prince Souvanna Vong was the leader of the rebels.

In November, 1957, the two junior half-brothers, as leaders of the government and the rebels, reached a political accord. They agreed to form a coalition government in which two cabinet posts (including the powerful Minister of Planning, Reconstruction, and Town Planning in charge of foreign aid) where given to Communists. They also agreed to incorporate the administration of the two northeastern provinces into the framework of the royal government; to incorporate the Pathet Lao army into the regular Lao army; to dissolve the Pathet Lao Movement and to replace it with a legalized party to be known as Neo Lao Hak Sat, or Laotian Patriotic Front; and to hold new elections under an extended electoral law for a government to convene in May, 1958.

In foreign affairs, the Laos were oriented towards their neighbors and kinsmen (and eternal enemies), the Thais. They shared little in common with the Vietnam "foreigners" on the other side of the mountains. They were exposed to Chinese, who swarmed over the border at will. Laos retained a lively respect for the French and kept alive its membership in the French Union. After Geneva, Americans made themselves prominent in Laos. The aid program—which in Laos was the highest per capita for any nation in the world—provided for some peaceful purposes like schools, health, transportation, and public administration. But more than that it created and sustained the entire army of Laos. In spite of which, Laos did not turn its back on neutralism. It cited the supreme wisdom of "our revered master, Buddha Sakyamuni," who taught: "The middle course is the course in which eyes will be opened and intelligence enlightened. It leads to peace, lucidity, and serenity."

— 9 —

THE PHILIPPINES

World War II. Within hours after Pearl Harbor, the skies of the Philippines were darkened by hundreds of Japanese planes. In one morning—December 8 on the Asian side of the international date line—the striking power of the United States was demolished. After days of bombing and approaching disaster, President Quezon and Vice-President Osmena transferred the Commonwealth government to Corregidor. Heartsick because of the suffering in his homeland, Quezon sent a radio request to President Roosevelt for immediate independence and neutralization. General MacArthur warned President Roosevelt, "You must figure on the complete destruction of this command—you must determine whether the mission of delay would be better furthered by the temporizing plan of Quezon or by my continued battle effort." The President replied to Quezon, "We will not relax until our forces return to drive out the last remnants of the invader from your soil." Quezon, choking in the dust and smoke, "swore to myself and the god of my ancestors that so long as I lived I would stand by America."

By patrol boat, submarine, and plane, the Commonwealth government managed to reach Australia and eventually Washington. Officials who were left behind, had to rely upon their own resources to deal with the victorious Japanese. Bataan surrendered in April, 1942; Corregidor in May; and the southern islands in June. Americans were interned or imprisoned. Filipinos had only the choice of becoming guerrillas or matching wits with the enemy in outward collaboration.

During three and a half years of occupation, the Filipinos were the bad boys of Southeast Asia in the eyes of Japan. No amount of intimidation or cajolery could induce the Filipinos to abandon their incorrigible urge to freedom. The Philippines were given "independence" in October, 1943. The Japanese-sponsored government dutifully allied itself with Japan and declared war on the United States. But no Philippine troops took the field, and no force could stop the flow of vital information from the hills to the liberation troops which assembled in the southwest Pacific.

The return to the Philippines seemed a distant dream not only for the fighting forces but also for the helpless millions who groaned under the cruelty of the occupation. When liberation came, the ecstatic taste of freedom quickly turned into the horror of the bombardment and sack of Manila. Freedom regained became paradise lost as mopping-up operations took a mounting toll of Philippine and American lives. When the Japanese retreated, they left in the Philippines an appalling wreckage of broken bodies and desolate spirits, of physical destruction and a shattered economy.

The Republic of the Philippines.   Never were birth
pangs more agonizing than those of the Republic of the
Philippines. President Quezon had died in exile, and President Osmena succeeded him. President Osmena had
waded ashore at Leyte with General MacArthur, and in
February, 1945, he returned his government to Manila.
He reconvened the Congress. Of twenty-four Senators,
seven were dead, and seven were in the hands of the
Counter Intelligence Corps. Of ninety-eight Representatives, seven had been arrested, twenty had been in the
puppet Assembly, and eleven had taken jobs under the
Japanese, while others were dead or missing. The government was helpless. Important decisions on all matters
were made by the army, which was preparing for the
invasion of Japan. With only token authority, President
Osmena had to make ready for independence, scheduled
for July 4, 1946.

He relied upon American policies as personified by the
new High Commissioner, Paul McNutt. The major problems were agrarian unrest, disposal of ex-enemy property,
investigation and trial of collaborators, reorganization of
the Philippine Constabulary, restoration of economic activity, and preparation for new elections. There was no
starvation—the army took care of that—but otherwise
chaos reigned. Time was required before American
promises for reconstruction and rehabilitation could be
fulfilled.

Elections were held on April 23, 1946, while many
parts of the country were still under the control of the
military. The candidates were President Osmena and
Eulogio Rodriguez for the old-time Nacionalistas, and
Manuel Roxas and Elpidio Quirino for the newly formed
Liberals, or Liberal wing of the Nacionalistas. The guerrillas and the Democratic Alliance stayed with President
Osmena. The Liberals—energized by the younger, more
dynamic Manuel Roxas, who had accepted a position
under the Japanese—gained the support of most Americans, the press, the landlord class, the church, and the
civil service. The issues were collaboration, personalities,
and alleged influence with the United States. The election itself was a travesty on the democratic process, and
it resulted in a Roxas-Quirino victory. The Liberals con-

trolled the Congress, prevented some victorious Nacionalistas from taking their seats, and thus gained the power to push through a controversial trade bill which the Americans insisted upon.

Independence was promised for July 4, 1946. The Philippines received independence exactly as promised, in spite of war and uncertainty. The American flag came down, and the Republic of the Philippines was born.

Descent to the Depths: 1946-1949. President Roxas was brilliant; he was expected to make the most of the skill of the Filipinos and American aid in reconstruction. He received immediate emergency loans, tax refunds, and more than half a billion dollars for the satisfaction of war damage claims and rehabilitation. The government tried halfheartedly to channel its windfall into beneficial agricultural and industrial development schemes, but government officials became too engrossed in the game of making quick profits. One was reported to have said: "Before we rehabilitate the country, let us rehabilitate ourselves." Humble people who received money wanted to buy pretty luxuries which they had been deprived of for years. Imports raced ahead of exports and dollars siphoned back into the United States. Production lagged, and taxes fell off. Danger signals warned of hard times ahead.

As an issue, collaboration disappeared. In January, 1948, President Roxas granted a general amnesty. His great problem was agrarian unrest. The peasant movement had fallen into the hands of the Communist-led Hukbalahap, or anti-Japanese Peoples Liberation Army. Its war record was impressive, but just the same the president branded the Huks as outlaws. The abuses of which they complained were not halted by bullets. The army and the constabulary were not equal to their job, and the countryside suffered from the undisciplined military, as well as from the Huks.

President Roxas remarshalled his forces. He initiated a land reform program and launched a new move for industrialization. He began financial reforms which led up to the creation of the Central Bank and the imposition of import and exchange controls. He died in office, and Quirino became president. Quirino gave his energies to reorganizing his political machine and winning the election in 1949. He was opposed by former President Laurel (under the Japanese) as standard bearer for the Nacionalistas. The election was marked by terror and mass frauds. Quirino won, but victory only served further to alienate the people from the government. The economy continued to deteriorate. At the time of the invasion of Korea, the Republic of the Philippines faced political and economic bankruptcy.

Improvement: The Quirino Administration, 1949-1953. In the summer of 1950, President Quirino invited the all-American Bell Economic Survey Mission to the Philippines. The Mission sounded an alarm for immediate action. In November, 1950, the Philippines and the United States agreed to an improvement program. The Philippines would reform land legislation and the tax system and would pass a minimum-wage law. The United States would grant $250,000,000 in loans over a five-year period.

The local law and order situation took a turn for the better, when the dynamic Ramon Magsaysay—former guerrilla captain, trucking operator, and congressman— was made Secretary of Defense. Magsaysay demonstrated his vigor and his political acumen in a successful campaign against the Huks. He brought a new sense of responsibility to the army. When he went after the Huks, he destroyed them or won them. He understood the harsh realities of poverty which drove men to rebellion. He held out hope for new life to those who would surrender. He broke the back of the Huk movement.

He soon overshadowed President Quirino with his popularity. The Quirino administration took credit for the restoration of order, but persistent graft and corruption made the administration more and more detestable. The press regularly headlined scandals in real estate deals, school supplies, Chinese immigration quotas, surplus property, crop loans, and import licenses. Whether from jealousy on the part of Quirino, or disgust or ambition on the part of Magsaysay, the two men came to a parting of the ways. The realistic political leaders of the Nacionalista party—Senators Rodriguez, Laurel, and Recto— came to an agreement with the rising young star, Magsaysay, the former Liberal. They gave him the Nacionalista nomination for the presidency in 1953 in exchange for his promise to consult them on appointments. Quirino insisted on running again. He wanted another chance to redeem his good name and the reputation of his party.

Ramon Magsaysay, 1953-1957. The Nacionalistas chose Carlos P. Garcia, an unspectacular, but dependable, party regular from the south as Magsaysay's running mate. The election produced new campaign tactics. A Committee for Free Elections worked for honesty at the ballot box. A Magsaysay-for-President movement helped create mass enthusiasm for "the guy." Magsaysay endeared himself to the common man. With an unfailing human touch, and barnstorming tirelessly from one end of the islands to the other, he won the hearts of the *barrios*. He broke the grip which the traditional combination of landlords and politicians had held on the electorate.

In office, Magsaysay invited "barefeet to the palace." He demanded an honest day's work and integrity from his appointees. He climaxed his drive for internal security with the surrender of Luis Taruc, the Huk Supremo. He went to work immediately for the welfare of tenants and poor farmers, offering them more land, loans at cheaper rates, advice on better marketing and production methods, more wells, and better highways. He set up a Complaints and Action Committee to go into the grievances of the little man. He appointed a presidential assistant for community development. He made preliminary moves towards the solution of pressing problems like industrialization. He geared his economic program to jobs and prices—factors which the people could understand. While pondering decisions he always asked, "How would this sound in Plaza Miranda?" (the Manila equivalent of Hyde Park). His critics were few, if passionate. They said he did not have the brains for big issues, that he occupied himself with small things. They said he leaned too much towards religion and the church; too little towards education and the public schools. The appropriation for the army increased under him. He had no foreign policy, it was charged, save dependence on the United States. (*See Reading No. 25.*)

On March 17, 1957, the Philippines lost a leader with a great heart, when his plane crashed against a mountain near Cebu. The new president, Carlos Garcia, said, "Our people feel lonely and orphaned; but Malacanan shall remain the palace of the people." Farmers, fishermen, and taxi drivers felt that they had been robbed of one to whom they could talk, one who really cared.

President Garcia. With Magsaysay gone, everybody eyed the presidency. Four teams entered the race in 1957. Carlos Garcia and Jose Laurel, Jr. for the incumbents; Jose Yulo and Diasdao Macapagal for the Liberal opposition; Manuel Manahan and Vicente Araneta for the Progressives, or self-styled heirs of Magsaysay; and Claro M. Recto and Lorenzo Tanada for the Nacionalista-Citizen's Party, the champions of the independents. The election was a national fiesta with bright lights and blatant huckstering. The candidates slugged it out with invective but shied away from issues. They courted the favor of the church and tried to seduce the electorate with promises. The voters responded with something novel in Philippine politics: a president, Garcia, of one party and a vice-president, Macapagal, of another. The Nacionalistas strengthened their control of the Senate and the House and pledged themselves to the continuation of the Magsaysay program for good government, better living, and peace.

Good government depended upon the central authorities. The national government at Manila controlled finances and appointments, and the executive branch controlled the national government. Too often the legislature acted as a mere rubber stamp. The habits of inefficiency, extravagance, and corruption clung to the politicians; these were relentlessly exposed by a vigorous free press. Specific abuses included useless junkets, nepotism, misuse of contingent funds, and unwarranted allocation of dollars. Law and order presented no immediate problem. Legislation was passed to outlaw the Communist Party and its militant arm, the Huks, and to prevent or counter Red infiltration into the unions. There would be peace in the countryside as long as the farmers received a decent price for their crops and a reasonable hope for government action in their behalf.

The main challenge to the Garcia-Macapagal administration was economic. Difficulties were age-old, passed
on from generation to generation since colonial times.
Improvements were slow, and it was a question whether
they kept ahead of the growing population. The fundamental problem was to raise the level of living for the
farmers—how to give them more income without boost-
ing the cost of rice for the poor consumers. The Garcia
formula was the obvious one: increase agricultural production and provide more jobs by industrialization. It was
urgent to find jobs for nearly two million unemployed.
The resources existed for significant industrial expansion, but not the managerial talent, the skilled-labor pool,
the electric power, or the transportation network. Foreign
investors held back pending an acceptable compromise
between their requirements and the nationalistic demands
for self-reliance and self-sufficiency. New factories were
built, hundreds of them, but they needed raw materials
from abroad. Under existing controls and current rates
of consumption, the Philippines paid more for imports
than their exports earned. Deficits were met by private
capital and dwindling government reserves. Pessimists
predicted "dirty weather ahead." Solvency and development meant an embarrassing reliance on foreign assistance. The matter of loans meant a careful weighing of
political consequences upon newly won independence.

Foreign Affairs. Since Roxas, the foreign policy
of the Philippines had been "frank, wholehearted and
open cooperation with the United States." Garcia said
that he would continue this policy. Mutual security called
for agreements on military bases, bilateral defense
treaties, and participation in SEATO. Trade relations
remained the same, with the Philippines selling most of
its products to the favored American market. At the
same time, the Philippines absorbed $150,000,000 in
United States government expenditures every year, of
which 15 per cent represented receipts under the assistance program.

Some Filipinos felt an increasing sense of indignity
over having to play the role of the "tail on the American
kite." They recognized the advantage of bases but argued
for recognition of their sovereignty and jurisdiction.

They said: "We do not want your air force officers thinking and acting as if they were on a base in Texas." They appreciated the catalytic effect of the American aid program, but they objected to its biased and exaggerated propaganda. They resented the underestimation of their own efforts in economic development. They questioned the costs, competence, and even the motives of some of the American administrators.

Some Filipinos flayed their officials who kowtowed to the United States. Filipinos in general applauded the frank statement of Ambassador Bohlen, "I expect the government of the Philippines to be just as assiduous in protecting its rights and interests as I am in protecting those of the United States." They demanded negotiation of each issue on its own merits, and not on sentimental appeals of past friendship or historical relations. They saw no anti-Americanism in demanding mutual respect and reciprocity in place of condescension.

Outside of relations with the United States, the Philippines stressed its role in the United Nations. It was the only charter member of the U. N. in Southeast Asia, and Ambassador Romulo had served as president of the General Assembly. The Philippines wanted nothing to do with Russia or mainland China, with neutralism, or with Asia for the Asiatics. It had to be alert for possible shifts in American policy. Regarding Japan, it wanted settlement of reparations payments and limited expansion of economic relations. Filipinos broadened the search for trade and investments among the nations of western Europe. Coups d'état in Thailand and chaos in Indonesia made them pay closer attention to their neighbors. They began to realize they were part of Southeast Asia.

TODAY'S WORLD IN SOUTHEAST ASIA

This book began with Southeast Asia's view of its place in today's world. It ends with the Southeast Asian thoughts about the outside world as it affects them. Seventy-five per cent of the people have no thoughts on the subject. Another 15 per cent, in the cities, derive their impressions from the foreigners they meet and the things they see. The remaining 10 per cent are no more unanimous or impartial in their views than their counterparts in the west. They interpret world affairs from the standpoint of themselves and the nations to which they owe allegiance.

The Legacy of History. Southeast Asians readily acknowledged their debt to the western world. Every country, even Thailand, owed its progress to foreign initiative. Foreigners created the plantations, developed the mines, and built the railroads and factories. They provided jobs for native workmen and offered opportunities for local capital, including Chinese and Indian. They brought to the east the welcome products of western machines—textiles in the old days, automobiles and air conditioners in the new. They purchased Southeast Asia's tropical products, even if they held one-crop economies at their mercy.

Southeast Asia felt the impact of political and scientific revolution in the west. It suffered in the wake of western wars, but it also shared the benefits of mankind's greatest medicinal discoveries. Its newly acquired nationalism owed a great deal to former colonial masters. Acknowledgment of the debt of the past did not detract one whit from the determination to subordinate the interests of the west to native interests and to live a future of its own making—whether brighter or darker—in independence and freedom.

Great Britain. Three hundred years of history die hard. The former colonies brought down the curtain on imperial rule, but they could not and would not eradicate the influences which survived. The exit of the French and Dutch, like the Portuguese and Spanish before them, meant the eclipse of their political power in Southeast Asia. Not so with the British. Great Britain, as a copartner with the United States and as the keystone of the Commonwealth, attained prestige as a stabilizer and peace preserver which was as effective in its way as the power it wielded in its heyday as the great empire-builder. It was not that Southeast Asians generated any love for the British; it was only that they regarded the British with a new respect. New nations with great problems gained a fresh appreciation of the achievement of colonial administration, and they liked the way in which the British gracefully bowed to the inevitable in liquidating their possessions. British Borneo and Hongkong were the exceptions. Asians discovered that the British were better neighbors as purveyors of services—merchants, bankers, shippers, insurance brokers, advisers, and technicians—than they had been as minions of empire. They hated the British in the Suez crisis as much as they hated the memory of the Burma wars, but in a new age their main concern shifted from Great Britain to the United States, Russia, China, and Japan.

Southeast Asia and the United States. The position of the United States in Asia changed with the atom bomb. Before then, America was the great symbol of revolution and independence; after that, it was the emblem of power. Americans stood alone as unmatchable representatives of the scientific age. Neither British nor French were accepted as the equal of Americans, let alone the Russians. The United States was regarded as the ultimate in technical know-how and industrial development. Her military power was beyond dispute. American ships had destroyed the Japanese navy, and GIs with science-fiction weapons had driven out the Japanese invaders. Every plane in the sky bore the unmistakable trade-mark of the United States.

In Asian eyes, power was not equated with greatness. The limits of power were constrained by the fuzziness of

American policy. (*See Reading No. 26.*) Asians lost confidence in the United States as the champion of the "free," after the compromises with hated colonialism in Indonesia and Indochina. With McCarthyism, Asians saw the United States lose its spirit of tolerance and easy optimism. They could not figure out how to adjust their own policies to a strong America which relied upon opportunism. They asked, "How can the United States vacillate so wildly in China? How can it forget overnight its hatred of Japan? How can it fight so bravely and quit so easily in Korea? How can it be so blind to everything else in its effort to contain communism? How can it squander so much on military aid and so little for humanitarian and social purposes? How can it be so careless of the sensibilities of Asians? How can it permit its policies to degenerate, in the words of Senator Mansfield, to a 'hodgepodge of sterile slogans and fumbling fear?' "

Asians lost confidence in the capacity of the United States to carry out the responsibilities of its power in world affairs. Mayor Lacson of Manila said in 1957, "Not for thirty years has friendship for the United States been at such a low ebb . . . It is not that I am anti-American. I am anti-stupidity. When the United States follows a policy I know to be stupid and shortsighted, I am against it." He was angered particularly by the extent of American aid to Japan. Americans were accused of failing to practice what they preached. Abroad, they preached the dignity of the individual and the rights of all men, at home they practised segregation. Secretary Dulles made headlines in Asia with his statement, "The purpose of the State Department is to look out for the interests of the United States. Whether we make friends, I do not care." Many intelligent Asians felt curiously relieved by his bluntness. In their view they would not be dragged to another brink of war for the interests of the United States presented to them as a moral crusade.

Southeast Asian reaction to American maneuvers in the cold war depended upon individual attitudes. (*See Reading No. 27.*) Some approved; others objected to the whole process of choosing sides. The allies of the United States welcomed military aid. The neutralists argued that only nonmilitary aid was compatible with peaceful coexistence. The Communists charged "American imperialism." The buyers of rice (Indonesia and the Philippines were glad for surplus agricultural commodities; the sellers of rice (Thailand and Burma) resented American dumping. (They objected to rice, but they bought milk and textiles.)

Southeast Asians reacted generally with skepticism to the overwhelming emphasis on the military aspects of the aid programs. Native soldiers—never held highly in esteem—were well taken care of. American-style uniforms enlivened parade grounds from Korea to Thailand. Oil storage facilities, vehicles, tanks, patrol boats, transport planes, and jet fighters all came from America. Joint United States Military Advisory Groups (JUSMAG) and United States Operations Missions (USOM) worked feverishly for mutual security. But Asians wondered about the creation of armies. Would they preserve the nation and contribute to stability, or would they make civil wars worse? Would military juntas give Southeast Asia the complexion of Latin America at its worst, or would alert young officers become civic leaders? As one Filipino asked, "Will these jokers work or will they play mahjong and cheat to keep the jeeps and cars to which they have become accustomed?"

American economic programs aroused a mixed chorus of praise and blame. They helped to stimulate agricultural production, social progress, and the growth of industries. Teachers, doctors, engineers, farmers, and surveyors worked at the grass roots, and they trained native helpers. President Diem called American aid "phenomenal." Elsewhere, approval was less enthusiastic. Asians emphasized that aid was extended in American self-interest and was therefore no cause for gratitude. They felt that too many mediocre Americans took an overseas assignment as an interesting experience or a good deal—as an excellent opportunity to see the world at government expense and to collect cheap, unusual souvenirs. Asians decried the waste, the rusting machines, and the useless projects which they also helped to pay for. They objected to the costly administrative machinery which struggled with strictly American problems like quarters, leaves, car pools, local procurement, commissary, Post

Exchange, and tax exemptions. They wished that programs had been more tailored to their own needs and desires. They resented most the American propaganda which came with aid. They said very clearly that their friendship and political decisions were not for sale.

Few in Southeast Asia had kind words to say for the United States Information Service (USIS) as an agency, or unkind words to say about the individuals employed. Hollywood movies were more popular than documentary films. *Time, Life,* and *Newsweek* attracted more readers than the *Free World*. News about the United States in local newspapers was more acceptable than the mimeographed handouts of the American Embassy. There was no lack of public relations personnel or available dollars to tell the American story. Friendly Asians suggested better, rather than more, activity, the substitution of thoughtfulness for platitudes, and a more lively concern for Southeast Asia than for anti-communism.

The USIS had always been plagued with the problems of race relations, but it faced an entirely new situation with the launching of the Soviet satellite. Sputnik—like the atom bomb before it—was spectacular. It acted as a catalyst for new attitudes towards the United States and Russia. Declining American prestige dipped to a new low. Asians no longer believed in the *unique* ability of the U. S. as the leader in science. There was no longer the feeling that the Communists were technically inferior. The great machines and gadgets of the U. S. continued to cause Asians to wonder—but most to wonder what Russia had in reserve.

Russia. Russia was the greatest source of Communist strength in Southeast Asia. Its industrialization record, real or fancied, was the accepted lodestar of the underdeveloped nations. The U.S.S.R. appropriated good words and phrases as its own: *democracy, camp of socialism, friend of nationalism, enemy of poverty, peace.* On November 17, 1957, it released two communiqués in Moscow which illustrated its propaganda methods. One was a joint declaration of basic laws and unity of aims signed by the party leaders of the Communist states (Jugoslavia abstained). It exuded confidence in the continued expansion of the united socialist (Communist) world under Soviet leadership. It called for the revival of popular fronts to win state power by constitutional means. It sought to regain the advantages of the Comintern and Cominform by advocating "more current discussion and concerted action in the joint struggle for common goals." The second communiqué was a peace manifesto signed by sixty-four Communist Parties which formally endorsed every aspect of Russian foreign policy.

Russia refrained from direct military intervention and overt aggression. It depended upon local armies to fight Communist battles. It relied upon well-organized local Communist Parties for propaganda and subversion or ordinary political tactics to gain favor and power. In economic policies, it looked as if the Soviet newcomers profited from the trials and errors of American experience. They talked about trade, not aid. Trade negotiations started with the purchase of Southeast Asia's surplus raw materials. Russia brought rice and rubber; it did not flood the market with competing goods. It then offered barter agreements for payments. It limited loans and grants to projects for which the need was obvious: a steel mill for Indonesia, a hospital for Cambodia, and a technical school for Burma. Russia was criticized for delivering inferior goods at high prices, for promising more than it could produce, but the objections to its economic program were slight as compared with the adverse criticisms of the United States.

China.   After the stabilization of the Peking regime, Southeast Asia had new worries about the Chinese minorities. The Chinese were everywhere, their shops "at the end of every jungle path." Suddenly the Chinese were not abandoned expatriates, but pampered nationals of a strong country. The indigenous populations became more restive about their potential fifth columns. They had not been perturbed by the diplomatic intercessions of Chiang Kai-shek and the National Government on Formosa, but they were alarmed by the possible success of Chou En-lai and his suave diplomacy.

As Peking gained in international prestige, more overseas Chinese political fence-sitters displayed the five-starred red flag of Communist China. The communism of China contributed in large measure to the victories of Ho

Chi Minh and to the emergency in Malaya. It explained the hesitancy in the national policies of Indonesia and Burma. It accounted for the sternness of the anti-Chinese legislation in the Philippines, Thailand, and South Vietnam. Native peoples feared the possible effects of a new burst of vitality from the Chinese mainland. They worried about Communist influence in the command of their local armies and the prospect of invasion from China itself. They could not entertain the peaceful overtures of Chou without precautions against his changing his tone.

Japan.   Southeast Asians also detected the increasing influence of Japan. The Japanese began to filter back into lands they had once occupied. Professors came on exchange grants, followed by experts to rehabilitate mines or salvage sunken ships. Traders brought cheap and intriguing goods to local bazaars. Brand new ships with the familiar "Maru" markings split the horizons of Southeast Asian waters. Beautiful posters of the Japan Air Lines put in their colorful bids for tours and travel. Japanese salesmen returned with brief cases and cameras. Enterprising moving picture producers imported stars and equipment for location shots.

After the formal establishment of peace, Japan sought to heal wounds with reparations. It joined in the Colombo Plan, in the activities of the United Nations, and opened its schools to hundreds of Asian students. It made available technical assistance through service contracts and joint enterprises. Its prime minister dared to think in imaginative terms for long-range assistance. According to the Kishi plan, the United States would lend dollars for a Southeast Asia Development Fund. Those dollars would be converted into farms and factories with Japanese labor and technical skill. Southeast Asia would prosper, and Japan would become a counterbalance to China. Japan would again assume the task of saving Asia from communism. Japan would serve as a bridge between East and West and would help the United States understand Asia. A typical Southeast Asian response was, "No, thank you, we prefer to help ourselves. We cannot see how you —a Japanese—can help the United States to understand us Filipinos who probably know the United States better than you do."

Regionalism and Internationalism. Southeast Asians hoped for useful benefits from participation in regional and international organizations. Regionalism was not very strong. An Asian-African bloc seemed like a more practical idea than Asia for the Asiatics, but it contained only a limited appeal. Asians had too many conflicting interests, and they had little in common, apart from their colonial associations. The struggle against something that was dead was of little value in moulding the shape of Asia to come. After Bandung, the Asians demonstrated the need of a specific irritant—like West Irian—to inspire a general reunion again.

It was quite different with regard to international organizations, particularly the Colombo Plan and the United Nations. The Colombo Plan received increasing support. It was conceived in 1950 as an instrument for the givers and receivers of economic assistance—primarily within the Commonwealth—to pool their experience. Its membership expanded to include more than twenty nations with interests in the Asian area. The Plan itself did not put up a dollar of assistance. Its chief functions were advice and coordination. Its council met in annual sessions to discuss progress and needs and to match assets and liabilities. From its deliberations came an ever expanding program of giving and receiving help, which in the Asian view met the psychological objections to the programs of the United States and Russia.

The United Nations enjoyed a good reputation in Southeast Asia. Politicians liked to be named as delegates to U. N. meetings, and they welcomed the activities of the United Nations in their respective countries. U. N. agencies performed good work—the Economic Commission for Asia and the Far East, the World Health Organization, the Childrens Emergency Fund, the Food and Agriculture Organization, the United Nations Educational Scientific and Cultural Organization, and the Technical Assistance Administration. Whether to prevent or heal a breach of the peace, or to administer economic help, Southeast Asians would have been glad for more, rather than less, of the United Nations. It catered to their ambition to be treated automatically as equals, and on exactly the same basis as the other sovereign nations.

Part II
READINGS

— Reading No. 1 —

SPIRIT OF MODERN ASIA, PRIME MINISTER NEHRU[1]

On April 24, 1955, at the closing session of the Bandung Conference of Asian-African nations, Prime Minister Nehru described the psychological attitudes of Asian nations. Although India is not part of Southeast Asia, the intellect of the Indian prime minister is respected throughout the region. At Bandung he expressed the sentiments of the assembled national leaders.

✔   ✔   ✔

. . . But, there is yet another spirit of Asia today. As we all know, Asia is no longer passive today; it has been passive enough in the past. It is no more a submissive Asia; it has tolerated submissiveness for so long. Asia of today is dynamic; Asia is full of life. . . . We are great countries in the world who rather like having freedom, if I may say so, without dictation. Well, if there is anything that Asia wants to tell them it is this: No dictation there is going to be in the future; no "yes-men" in Asia, I hope, or in Africa. We have had enough of that in the past. We value friendship of the great countries and if I am to play my part, I should like to say that we sit with the great countries of the world as brothers, be it in Europe or America. It is not in any spirit of hatred or dislike or aggressiveness with each other in regard to Europe or America, certainly not. We send to them our greetings, all of us here, and we want to be

[1] George McTurnan Kahin, *The Asian-African Conference,* Bandung, Indonesia, April, 1955 (Ithaca: Cornell University Press, 1956), pp. 73-75.

friends with them, to cooperate with them. But we shall only cooperate in the future as equals; there is no friendship when nations are not equal, when one has to obey the other and when one dominates the other. That is why we raise our voice against domination and colonialism from which, many of us, have suffered so long and that is why we have to be very careful to see that any other form of domination does not come our way. Therefore, we want to be friends with the West and friends with the East and friends with everybody because if there is something that may be called an approach to the minds and spirit of Asia, it is one of toleration and friendship and cooperation, not one of aggressiveness. . . .

I realise, as the Prime Minister of Burma said, that we cannot exercise tremendous influence over the world. Our influence will grow, no doubt. . . . But whether our influence is great or small, it must be exercised in the right direction, in an intelligent direction, in a direction which has integrity of purpose and ideals and objectives as shown in our Resolution. It represents the ideals of Asia, it represents the new dynamism of Asia, because if it does not represent that what are we then? Are we copies of Europeans or Americans or Russians? What are we? We are Asians or Africans. We are none else. If we are camp followers of Russia or America or any other country of Europe, it is, if I may say so, not very creditable to our dignity, our new independence, our new freedom, our new spirit and our new self-reliance.

THE ASIAN-AFRICAN CONFERENCE, BANDUNG, INDONESIA, 1955[1]

In 1955 representatives of twenty-nine diverse nations of Asia and Africa met in Bandung, West Java, to discuss and deliberate upon matters of common concern. On April 24 they agreed upon the communiqué which reads substantially as follows.

✓   ✓   ✓

A. *Economic Cooperation*

1. The Asian-African Conference recognized the urgency of promoting economic development in the Asian-African region. There was general desire for economic cooperation among the participating countries on the basis of mutual interest and respect for national sovereignty. The proposals with regard to economic cooperation within the participating countries do not preclude either the desirability or the need for cooperation with countries outside the region, including the investment of foreign capital. It was further recognized that the assistance being received by certain participating countries from outside the region, through international or under bilateral arrangements, had made a valuable contribution to the implementation of their development programmes. . . .

B. *Cultural Cooperation*

1. . . . The peoples of Asia and Africa are now animated by a keen and sincere desire to renew their old

Extracts from the final communiqué. Most conveniently found in George McTurnan Kahin, *op. cit.*, pp. 76-85.

cultural contacts and develop new ones in the context of the modern world . . .

C. *Human Rights and Self-determination*

1. The Asian-African Conference declared its full support of the fundamental principles of Human Rights as set forth in the Charter of the United Nations . . . (and) of the principles of self-determination of peoples and nations as set forth in the Charter of the United Nations . . .

2. The Asian-African Conference deplored the policies and practices of racial segregation and discrimination which form the basis of government and human relations in large regions of Africa and in other parts of the world . . .

D. *Problems of Dependent Peoples*

1. . . . The Conference is agreed:

(a) in declaring that colonialism in all its manifestations is an evil which should speedily be brought to an end.

(b) in affirming that the subjection of peoples to alien subjugation, domination, and exploitation constitutes a denial of fundamental human rights, is contrary to the Charter of the United Nations and is an impediment to the promotion of world peace and cooperation;

(c) in declaring its support of the cause of freedom and independence for all such people, and

(d) in calling upon the powers concerned to grant freedom and independence to all such peoples.

2. . . . the Asian-African Conference declared its support of the rights of the people of Algeria, Morocco, and Tunisia to self-determination and independence and urged the French Government to bring about a peaceful settlement of the issue without delay.

E. *Other Problems*

1. . . . the Asian-African Conference declared its support of the rights of the Arab people of Palestine and called for the implementation of the United Nations Res-

olutions on Palestine and the achievement of the peaceful settlement of the Palestine question . . .

2. The Asian-African Conference, . . . supported the position of Indonesia in the case of West Irian based on the relevant agreements between Indonesia and the Netherlands. . . .

3. The Asian-African Conference supported the position of Yemen in the case of Aden and the southern parts of Yemen known as the protectorates. . . .

F. *Promotion of World Peace and Cooperation*

1. The Asian-African Conference . . . considered that for effective cooperation for world peace, membership in the United Nations should be universal, called on the Security Council to support the admission of all those states which are qualified for membership in terms of the Charter. In the opinion of the Asian-African Conference, the following among participating countries, viz: Cambodia, Ceylon, Japan, Jordan, Libya, Nepal, a unified Vietnam were so qualified. . . .

G. *Declaration on the Promotion of World Peace and Cooperation*

. . . nations should practise tolerance and live together in peace with one another . . . on the basis of the following principles:

1. Respect for fundamental human rights and for the purposes and principles of the Charter of the United Nations.

2. Respect for the sovereignty and territorial integrity of all nations.

3. Recognition of the equality of all races and the equality of all nations large and small.

4. Abstention from intervention or interference in the internal affairs of another country.

5. Respect for the right of each nation to defend itself singly or collectively, in conformity with the Charter of the United Nations.

6. (a) Abstention from the use of arrangements of collective defence to serve the particular interests of any of the big powers. (b) Abstention by any country from exerting pressures on other countries.

7. Refraining from acts or threats of aggression or the use of force against the territorial integrity or political independence of any country.

8. Settlement of all international disputes by peaceful means, such as negotiation, conciliation, arbitration or judicial settlement, as well as other peaceful means of the parties own choice, in conformity with the Charter of the United Nations.

9. Promotion of mutual interests and cooperation.

10. Respect for justice and international obligations. . . .

Bandung, 24th April, 1955

— Reading No. 3 —

SOUTHEAST ASIA COLLECTIVE DEFENSE TREATY AND PACIFIC CHARTER, 1954[1]

After the defeat of the French in Indochina and the conclusion of the armistice arrangements at Geneva on July 20, 1954, representatives of Australia, France, New Zealand, Pakistan, the Philippines, Thailand, the United Kingdom, and the United States met in Manila on September 6 to "strengthen the fabric of peace and freedom and to uphold the principles of democracy, individual liberty and the rule of law, and to promote the economic well-being and development of all peoples in the Treaty area." They signed a Collective Defense Treaty and a Pacific Charter, which Nehru called acts of anger against Geneva but which Secretary Dulles called potential bulwarks against the spread of communism.

[1] Department of State *Bulletin,* XXXI, No. 795, September 20 1954, 393-396.

SOUTHEAST ASIA COLLECTIVE
DEFENSE TREATY

ARTICLE I. The Parties undertake . . . to refrain in their international relations from the threat or use of force in any manner inconsistent with the purposes of the United Nations.

ARTICLE II. . . . the Parties . . . will maintain and develop their individual and collective capacity to resist armed attack and to prevent and counter subversive activities directed from without against their territorial integrity and political stability.

ARTICLE III. The Parties undertake to strengthen their free institutions and to cooperate with one another in the further development of economic measures. . . .

ARTICLE IV. 1. Each Party recognizes that aggression by means of armed attack in the treaty area against any of the Parties or against any State or territory which the Parties by unanimous agreement may hereafter designate, would endanger its own peace and safety, and agrees that it will in that event act to meet the common danger in accordance with its constitutional processes. Measures taken under this paragraph shall be immediately reported to the Security Council of the United Nations.

2. If, in the opinion of any of the Parties, the inviolability or the integrity of the sovereignty or political independence of any Party in the treaty area or of any other State or territory to which the provisions of paragraph 1 of this Article from time to time apply is threatened in any way other than by armed attack or is affected or threatened by any fact or situation which might endanger the peace of the area, the Parties shall consult immediately in order to agree on the measures which should be taken for the common defense.

3. It is understood that no action on the territory of any State designated by unanimous agreement under paragraph 1 of this Article or on any territory so designated shall be taken except at the invitation or with the consent of the Government concerned.

ARTICLE VIII. As used in this Treaty, the 'treaty area' is the general area of Southeast Asia, including also the entire territories of the Asian Parties, and the general area of the Southwest Pacific not including the Pacific area north of 21 degrees 30 minutes north latitude . . .

Understanding of the United States of America

The United States of America in executing the present Treaty does so with the understanding that its recognition of the effect of aggression and armed attack and its agreement with reference thereto in Article IV, paragraph 1, apply only to Communist aggression, but affirms that in the event of other aggression or armed attack it will consult under the provisions of Article IV, paragraph 2.

PROTOCOL

Designation of States and Territory as to which Provisions of Article IV and Article III are to be applicable

The Parties to the Southeast Asia Collective Defense Treaty unanimously designate for the purposes of Article IV of the Treaty the States of Cambodia and Laos and the free territory under the jurisdiction of the State of Vietnam . . .

THE PACIFIC CHARTER

The Delegates . . . Do hereby proclaim:

First, in accordance with the provisions of the United Nations Charter, they uphold the principle of equal rights and self-determination of peoples, and they will earnestly strive by every peaceful means to promote the self-government and to secure the independence of all countries whose people desire it and are able to undertake its responsibilities;

Second, they are each prepared to continue taking effective practical measures to ensure conditions favorable to the orderly achievement of the foregoing purposes in accordance with their constitutional processes;

Third, they will continue to cooperate in the economic, social, and cultural fields in order to promote higher living standards, economic progress and social well-being in this region;

Fourth, as declared in the Southeast Asia Collective Defense Treaty, they are determined to prevent or counter by appropriate means any attempt in the treaty area to subvert their freedom or to destroy their sovereignty or territorial integity.

Proclaimed at Manila, this eighth day of September, 1954.

— Reading No. 4 —

TREATY BETWEEN THE ENGLISH EAST INDIA COMPANY AND THE "KING OF QUEDAH," APRIL 20, 1791[1]

In 1786 Francis Light, master of a sailing ship from India to the Malay peninsula, obtained the cession of the island of Penang from the "King of Quedah." This was the first territorial possession of the British in Southeast Asia. Ignoring the insistent demands of the aforesaid king for the company's protection and the king's quasi-vassal relationship to the king of Siam, Light concluded the following treaty of peace and friendship.

↗   ↗   ↗

In the Hegira of our Prophet, 1205, year Dalakir, on the 16th of moon Saban, on the day Ahat (20 April 1791)

Whereas on this date, this writing showeth that the Governor of Pulo Penang, vakeel of the English Company, concluded peace and friendship with His Highness, Iang de per Tuan of Quedah, and all his great officers and ryots of the two countries, to live in peace by sea and land, to continue as long as the Sun and Moon give light: the Articles of Agreement are:—

ARTICLE 1. The English Company will give to His Highness, the Iang de per Tuan of Quedah, six thousand

---

[1] *Treaties and Engagements with the Native States of the Malay Peninsula before 1860.* (No author, date, or place of publication.) Found in the Raffles Library, Singapore, p. 64.

Spanish Dollars every year, for as long as the English shall continue in possession of Pulo Penang.

ARTICLE 2. His Highness, the Iang de per Tuan, agrees that all kinds of provisions wanted for Pulo Penang, the ships of war, and the Company's ships, may be bought at Quedah, without impediment, or being subject to any duty.

ARTICLE 3. All slaves running from Quedah to Pulo Penang, or from Pulo Penang to Quedah, shall be returned to their owners.

ARTICLE 4. All persons in debt running from their creditors from Quedah to Pulo Penang or from Pulo Penang to Quedah, if they do not pay their debts, their persons shall be delivered over to their creditors.

ARTICLE 5. The Iang de per Tuan will not allow Europeans of any other nation to settle in any part of his country.

ARTICLE 6. The Company shall not receive any persons committing high treason or rebellion against the Iang de per Tuan.

ARTICLE 7. All persons committing murder, running from Quedah to Pulo Penang or from Pulo Penang to Quedah, shall be apprehended and returned in bonds.

ARTICLE 8. All persons stealing chops (forgery) to be given up likewise.

ARTICLE 9. All persons, enemies to the English Company, the Iang de per Tuan shall not supply them with provisions.

These nine articles are settled and concluded, and peace is made between the Iang de per Tuan and the English Company; Quedah and Pulo Penang shall be as one country.

This done and completed by Toonkoo Sheriff Mahomed, the Toonkoo Allang Ibrahim, and Datoo Pengawa Telebone, vakeels, on the part of the Iang de per Tuan, and given to the Governor of Pulo Penang, vakeel for the English Company. In this agreement, whoever departs from any part herein written, God will punish and destroy; to him there shall be no health.

The seals of Sheriff Mahomed and Toonkoo Allang Ibrahim, and Datoo Pengawa Telebone, are put to this writing, with each person's handwriting.

Transcribed by Hakim Bunder, Pulo Penang.

Signed, sealed, and executed in Fort Cornwallis, on Prince of Wales' Island, this 1st day of May, in the year of our Lord 1791.

A true translation.

(Signed) F. LIGHT

— Reading No. 5 —

THE ACQUISITION OF SINGAPORE, 1819[1]

On February 6, 1819, the energetic British public servant, Sir Thomas Stamford Raffles, accomplished one of the great bargains of history—the purchase, for a pittance, of the island of Singapore. Since that date, Raffles and Singapore have symbolized the British position in Southeast Asia. The agreement which follows is perhaps the prime exhibit in the arguments for and against the imperialism of the west.

✓   ✓   ✓

Treaty of Friendship and Alliance concluded between the Honourable Sir Thomas Stamford Raffles, Lieutenant-Governor of Fort Marlborough and its dependencies, Agent to the Most Noble Francis, Marquis of Hastings, Governor-General of India, &c, &c, &c., for the Honourable English East India Company, on the one part, and their Highness Sultan Hussain Mahummed Shah, Sultan of Johore, and Datoo Tumungong Sri Maharajah Abdul-Rahman, Chief of Singapore and its dependencies, on the other part.

ARTICLE 1. The preliminary Articles of Agreement

[1] *Treaties and Engagements with the Native States of the Malay Peninsula before 1860, op. cit.* p. 19.

entered into on the 30th of January 1819, by the Honourable Sir Stamford Raffles, on the part of the English East India Company and by Datoo Tumungong Sri Maharajah Abdul-Rahman, Chief of Singapore and its dependencies, for himself and for Sultan Hussain Mahummed Shah, Sultan of Johore, are hereby entirely approved, ratified and confirmed by His Highness, the aforesaid Sultan Mahummed Shah.

ARTICLE 2. In furtherance of the objects contemplated in the said Preliminary Agreement, and in compensation of any and all the advantages which may be foregone now or hereafter by His Highness Sultan Hussain Mahummed Shah, Sultan of Johore, in consequence of the stipulations of this Treaty, the Honourable English East India Company agree and engage to pay to his aforesaid Highness the sum of Spanish Dollars five thousand annually, for, and during the time that the said Company may, by virtue of this Treaty, maintain a factory or factories on any part of His Highness' hereditary dominions, and the said Company further agree to afford their protection to His Highness aforesaid as long as he may continue to reside in the immediate vicinity of the places subject to their authority. It is however clearly explained to and understood by His Highness, that the English Government, in entering into this Alliance, and in thus engaging to afford protection to His Highness, is to be considered in no way bound to interfere with the internal politics of his States, or engaged to assert or maintain the authority of His Highness by force of arms.

ARTICLE 3. His Highness, Datoo Tumungong Sri Maharajah Abdul-Rahman, Chief of Singapore and its dependencies, having by preliminary Articles of Agreement entered into on the 30th of January, 1819, granted his full permission to the Honourable English East India Company to establish a factory or factories at Singapore, or on any other part of His Highness' dominions, and the said Company, having, in recompense and in return for the said grant, settled on His Highness the yearly sum of Spanish Dollars three thousand, and having received His Highness into their alliance and protection, all and every part of the said Preliminary Articles is hereby confirmed.

ARTICLE 4. His Highness the Sultan Mahummed Shah, Sultan of Johore, and His Highness Datoo Tumungong Sri Maharajah Abdul-Rahman, Chief of Singapore, engage and agree to aid and assist the Honourable English East India Company against all enemies that may assail the factory or factories of the said Company, established or to be established, in the dominions of their said Highnesses respectively.

ARTICLE 5. His Highness the Sultan Hussain Mahummed Shah, Sultan of Johore and His Highness Datoo Tumungong Sri Maharajah Abdul-Rahman, Chief of Singapore, agree, promise and bind themselves, their heirs and successors, that for so long a time as the Honourable, the English East India Company, shall continue to hold the factory or factories on any part of the dominions subject to the authority of their Highnesses aforesaid, and shall continue to afford to their Highnesses support and protection, they, their said Highnesses, will not enter into any treaty with any other nation, and will not admit or consent to the settlement in any part of their dominions of any other power, European or American.

ARTICLE 6. All persons belonging to the English factory or factories, or who shall hereafter desire to place themselves under the protection of its flag, shall be duly registered and considered as subject to the British authority.

ARTICLE 7. The mode of administrating justice to the native population shall be subject to future discussion and arrangement between the contracting parties, as this will necessarily, in a great measure, depend on the laws and usages of the various tribes who may be expected to settle in the vicinity of the English factory.

ARTICLE 8. The port of Singapore is to be considered under the immediate protection and subject to the regulations of the British authorities.

ARTICLE 9. With regard to the Duties which it may hereafter be deemed necessary to levy on goods, merchandize, boats or vessels, His Highness Datoo Tumungong Sri Maharajah Abdul-Rahman is to be entitled to a moiety or full half of all the amount collected from native vessels.

The expenses of the port and of the collection of Duties is to be defrayed by the British Government.

Done and concluded at Singapore, this 6th day of February, in the year of our Lord 1819 answering to the 19th day of the month Rabi-al-Ahkir, and year of the Hejira 1234.

(Signed) T. S. RAFFLES
Agent to the Most Noble, the Governor-General for the States of Rhio, Singapore and Johore.

— Reading No. 6 —

MY LAST FAREWELL—DR. JOSÉ RIZAL, 1896[1]

Seldom can a nation boast a more perfect martyr than the great Filipino doctor, linguist, novelist, poet, and patriot—Dr. José Rizal. The world's literature is the richer for his heart-felt message written within the shadow of death in his prison cell at Fort Santiago in Manila. His poem was smuggled to the outside world in a little alcohol lamp given by Dr. Rizal to his sister on the eve of his execution, December 30, 1896, by a Spanish firing squad.

↑   ↑   ↑

Farewell, dear fatherland, clime of the sun caress'd,
Pearl of the Orient seas, our Eden lost!
Gladly now I give to thee this faded life's best,
And were it brighter, fresh, or more blest,
Still would I give it thee, nor count the cost.
On the field of battle, 'mid the frenzy of fight
Others have given their lives, without doubt or heed;
The place matters not—cypress or laurel or lily white,

[1] English translation by Charles Derbyshire, in Jaime C. De Veyra, *"El Ultimo Adios" de Rizal* (Manila: Bureau of Printing, 1946).

Scaffold or open plain, combat or martyrdom's plight,
'Tis ever the same, to serve our home and country's need.
I die just when I see the dawn break,
Through the gloom of night, to herald the day;
And if color is lacking my blood thou shalt take,
Pour'd out at need for thy dear sake,
To dye with its crimson the waking ray.

My dreams, when life first opened to me,
My dreams, when the hope of youth beat high,
Were to see thy lov'd face, O gem of the Orient sea,
From gloom and grief, from care and sorrow free;
No blush on thy brow, no tear in thine eye.

Dream of my life, my living and burning desire;
All hail; cries the soul that is now to take flight;
All hail! And sweet it is for thee to expire;
To die for thy sake, that thou mays't aspire;
And sleep in thy bosom eternity's long night.

If over my grave some day thou seest grow,
In the grassy sod, a humbled flower,
Draw it to thy lips and kiss my soul so,
While I feel on my brow in the cold tomb below,
The touch of thy tenderness, thy breath's warm power.

Let the moon beam over me soft and serene,
Let the dawn shed over me its radiant flashes,
Let the wind with sad lament over me keen;
And if on my cross a bird should be seen,
Let it trill there its hymn of peace to my ashes.

Let the sun draw vapors up to the sky,
And heavenward in purity bear my tardy protest;
Let some kind soul o'er my untimely fate sigh,
And in the still evening a prayer be lifted on high
From thee, O my country, that in God I may rest. . . .

Pray for all those that hapless have died,
For all who have suffered the unmeasur'd plain;
For our mothers that bitterly their woes have cried;
For widows and orphans, for captives by torture tried;
And then for thyself that redemption thou may'st gain.

And when the dark night wraps the graveyard around,
With only the dead in their vigil to see;
Break not my repose or the mystery profound,
And perchance thou may'st hear a sad hymn resound;
'Tis I, O my country, raising a song unto thee.

When even my grave is remembered no more,
Unmark'd by never a cross nor a stone;
Let the plow sweep through it, the spade turn it o'er,
That my ashes may carpet thy earthly floor,
Before into nothingness at last they are blown.
Then will oblivion bring me no care,
As over thy vales and plains I sweep,
Throbbing and cleansed in thy space and air,
With color and light, with song and lament I fare,
Ever repeating the faith that I keep.
My Fatherland adored, that sadness to my sorrow lends,
Beloved Filipinas, hear now my last good bye!
I give thee all, parents and kindred and friends;
For I go where no slave before the oppressor bends,
Where faith can never kill, and God reigns e'er on high!
Farewell to you all, from my soul torn away,
Friends of my childhood in the home dispossessed!
Give thanks that I rest from the wearisome day!
Farewell to thee, too, sweet friend that lightened my way;
Beloved creatures all, farewell! In death there is rest!

— Reading No. 7 —

PRESIDENT MCKINLEY'S INSTRUCTIONS TO THE PHILIPPINE COMMISSION, APRIL 7, 1900[1]

President McKinley instructed his Secretary of War, Elihu Root, that the Commissioners to the Philippine Islands were to continue and perfect the work of organizing and establishing civil government already commenced by the military authorities. These instructions illustrate the liberal spirit with which the government of the United States approached the problems of its newly acquired and distant possession overseas.

✓   ✓   ✓

In all the forms of government and administrative provisions which they are authorized to prescribe, the commission should bear in mind that the government which they are establishing is designed not for our satisfaction, or for the expression of our theoretical views, but for the happiness, peace, and prosperity of the people of the Philippine Islands, and the measures adopted should be made to conform to their customs, their habits, and even their prejudices, to the fullest extent consistent with the accomplishment of the indispensable requisites of just and effective government.

[1] Reports of the Philippine Commission, the Civil Governor, and the Heads of the Executive Departments of the Civil Government of the Philippine Islands (1900-1903), Bureau of Insular Affairs, War Department (Washington: Government Printing Office, 1904), pp. 1-11.

At the same time the commission should bear in mind, and the people of the islands should be made plainly to understand, that there are certain great principles of government which have been made the basis of our governmental system which we deem essential to the rule of law and the maintenance of individual freedom, and of which they have, unfortunately, been denied the experience possessed by us; that there are also certain practical rules of government which we have found to be essential to the preservation of these great principles of liberty and law, and that these principles and these rules of government must be established and maintained in their islands for the sake of their liberty and happiness, however much they may conflict with the customs or laws of procedure with which they are familiar. . . .

(These inviolable rules are) That no person shall be deprived of life, liberty, or property without due process of law; that private property shall not be taken for public use without just compensation; that in all criminal prosecutions the accused shall enjoy the right to a speedy and public trial; . . . that no law shall be passed abridging the freedom of speech or of the press, or the rights of the people to peaceably assemble and petition the government for a redress of grievances; that no law shall be made respecting an establishment of religion, or prohibiting the free exercise thereof, and that the free exercise and enjoyment of religious profession and worship without discrimination or preference shall forever be allowed . . . that no form of religion and no minister of religion shall be forced upon any community or upon any citizen of the islands; that upon the other hand no minister of religion shall be interfered with or molested in following his calling, and that the separation between state and church shall be real, entire, and absolute. . . .

It will be the duty of the commission to promote and extend, and, as they find occasion, to improve, the system of education already inaugurated by the military authorities. In doing this they should regard as of first importance the extension of a system of primary education which shall be free to all, and which shall tend to fit the people for the duties of citizenship and for the ordinary avocations of a civilized community. This instruction should be given in the first instance in every part of the islands in the language of the people. In view of the great number of languages spoken by the different tribes, it is especially important to the prosperity of the islands that a common medium of communication may be established, and it is obviously desirable that this medium should be the English language. Especial attention should be at once given to affording full opportunity to all the people of the islands to acquire the use of the English language.

Upon all officers and employees of the United States, both civil and military, should be impressed a sense of the duty to observe not merely the material but the personal and social rights of the people of the islands, and to treat them with the same courtesy and respect for their personal dignity which the people of the United States are accustomed to require from each other. . . .

(A) high and sacred . . . obligation rests upon the Government of the United States to give protection for property and life, civil and religious freedom, and wise, firm, and unselfish guidance in the paths of peace and prosperity to all the people of the Philippine Islands. I charge this commission to labor for the full performance of this obligation, which concerns the honor and conscience of their country, in the firm hope that through their labors all the inhabitants of the Philippine Islands may come to look back with gratitude to the day when God gave victory to American arms at Manila and set their land under the sovereignty and the protection of the people of the United States.

WILLIAM McKINLEY

— Reading No. 8 —

OUT OF EXILE, 1934-1942— SOETAN SJAHRIR[1]

At the age of twenty-five, Sjahrir—later prime minister of his country and founder of the Indonesian Socialist Party—was jailed by the Dutch. He was successively interned in New Guinea and exiled to the Banda Islands. During this difficult period of eight years, his letters reveal a spiritual treasure house which the Dutch to their own detriment failed to discover and to exploit.

December 9, 1934. . . .

It was as though I were recalled to my people when I received the banishment sentence; to my people and to everything that ties me to the destiny and suffering of these millions. My personal grief is finally only a small part of that greater, general suffering, and it is just this that is my deepest and strongest bond. And now, perhaps just when I have to renounce what I love best in the world, now I feel myself more firmly and indissolubly bound to my people than ever before!

We have so often misunderstood one another, that people and I. I have been too abstract for my people, too far removed from the framework of their concepts, too "Western." They have been, for me, too inert. They have often made me despair at their lack of will and their misconceptions; angry and impatient at their petty faults. They filled me sometimes even with bitterness, but now I know that their destiny and the goal of

[1] Soetan Sjahrir, *Out of Exile*. Translated, with an introduction, by Charles Wolf, Jr. (New York: the John Day Company, 1949).

my life are one; we were and we are still mutually bound to each other. Now that my people require from me the dissolution and the destruction of my personal happiness, the separation from my loved ones, now all my sorrow disappears, and there remains only my deep feeling of belonging and alliance to this downtrodden people of mine. (*Page 33*.)

December 31, 1936.

For me, the West signifies forceful, dynamic, and active life. It is a sort of Faust that I admire, and I am convinced that only by a utilization of this dynamism of the West can the East be released from its slavery and subjugation.

The West is now teaching the East to regard life as a struggle and a striving, as an active movement to which the concept of tranquillity must be subordinated. Goethe teaches us to love striving for the sake of striving, and in such a concept of life there is progress, betterment, and enlightenment. The concept of striving is not, however, necessarily connected with destruction and plunder as we now find it. On the contrary, even in Faust, striving and struggle have the implication of constructive work, of undertaking great projects for the benefit of humanity. In this sense, they signify a struggle against nature, and that is the essence of struggle: man's attempt to subdue nature and to rule it by his will. The forms that the struggle take indicate the development and refinement of the individuals who are engaged in the effort.

What we need is not rest—or death—but a higher form of living and of striving. We must extend and intensify life, and raise and improve the goals toward which we strive. This is what the West has taught us, and this is what I admire in the West despite its brutality and its coarseness. I would even take this brutality and coarseness as accompanying features of the new concept of life that the West has taught us. I would even accept capitalism as an improvement upon the much famed wisdom and religion of the East. For it is precisely this wisdom and religion that make us unable to understand the fact that we have sunk to the lowest depths to which man can descend: we have sunk to slavery and to enduring subjugation.

What we in the East admire most in the West is its indestructible vitality, its love for life and for the fulfillment of life. Every vital young man and young woman in the East ought to look toward the West, for he or she can learn only from the West to regard himself or herself as a center of vitality capable of changing and bettering the world. (*Page 144 ff.*)

March 12, 1937.

Many Europeans long for the East, which signifies to them tranquillity and reflection. In reality, the East is no longer that promised land of peace of mind and spirit. . . . There is no doubt that the people here are calmer and more easy going. But is it proper to exalt a constrained and far from pleasant situation of poverty and slavery as an ideal, simply by referring to it as "carefreeness" and "moral superiority"? . . .

I know only too well what the Eastern attributes, so admired by the Westerner really are. I know that those attributes are molded and nourished only by the hierarchical relationship of a feudal society—a society in which a small group possesses all the materials and intellectual wealth, and the vast majority live in squalor, and are made acquiescent by religion and philosophy in place of sufficient food. . . .

People who have been indigent for generations have indeed become well versed in Eastern life . . . And now there are many Westerners who are envious of these people, because they themselves have forgotten what rest is. But they lose sight of one other vital fact, and that is that this sort of "art" can be developed and applied only under the heel of a ruler, and that it exemplifies only the virtue of endurance and adaptation. And even here, the fact again appears that life is stronger than all negation, because the negation itself is in the service of life. The East's negation of life is really only an adaptation that makes an unbearable life bearable.

That the ruler envies the slave is, again, understandable. For tolerance and endurance are indeed real attributes, and in a certain sense one can truly say that the slave has cultivated the art of life—that is the art of self-adaptation—more fully than his master. . . . (*Page 159 ff.*)

March 25, 1938.

I have now come to the conclusion that the situation in the world has changed so much that opposition to the Dutch rule can no longer be the primary task of nationalist propaganda or of the nationalist movement itself. . . . It is now clear that we must take a stand in the same camp as Holland. More profound antitheses have now come to the fore, which overshadow and deprecate the conflict between Holland and Indonesia. . . .

There must be many changes in these Netherlands Indies before there can be any talk of real cooperation— that is cooperation without any evasion of reality. In the first place, there must be a moral revolution among the Netherlanders. In the second place, there must be a basic psychological change among the Indonesians themselves. They must free themselves of their distrust, fear and hate, and of their collective inferiority complex. . . .

In practice this psychological alteration will have organizational consequences. There will be an acceleration in the so-called "ethical policy," according to which the Indonesian people—as high a percentage as possible at present, and particularly the literates among them and their representatives, the intellectuals—will acquire real responsibility for the running of the country by joint government, and by representation in all governing bodies. This is the direct political prerequisite for cooperation. . . . (Cooperation) is feasible only if their is *equal responsibility* on both sides. It is possible only if there is equal moral and political stature on both sides.

The old, dear cant of the rulers that "the Indonesians are politically immature and for the present must not be concerned with political matters," will have to be discarded. . . . That same people which has hitherto been kept as far away as possible from government affairs must now be consciously drawn into them. That people must be made politically conscious. Its political interest must be stimulated and maintained.

And all this *shall* happen. The question is only whether it will take place from now on, regularly and according to plan, or suddenly, as a surprise and an eruption brought about by circumstances. (*Page 209 ff.*)

— Reading No. 9 —

JAPAN'S PRINCIPLES OF GREATER EAST ASIA, NOVEMBER 5, 1943[1]

The power and the ideas of Japan dominated South-east Asia for a brief moment of glory after the opening campaigns of World War II. The "independent" allies of Japan—Manchukuo, China, Thailand, Burma, and the Philippines—assembled in Tokyo in a conference of Greater East Asiatic nations, and issued the following joint declaration. The sentiments of this declaration might have prepared the way for more permanent cooperation between Japan and its neighbors, had it not been for the spirit of arrogance and the bitter memories of war with which this document is associated.

✦   ✦   ✦

It is the basic principle for the establishment of world peace that the nations of the world have each its proper place and enjoy prosperity in common through mutual aid and assistance. The U.S.A. and the British Empire have in seeking their own prosperity oppressed other nations and peoples. Especially in East Asia they indulged in insatiable aggression and exploitation and sought to satisfy their inordinate ambition of enslaving the entire region, and finally they came to menace seriously the

[1]Ministry of Greater East Asiatic Nations, *Addresses before the Assembly of Greater East Asiatic Nations* (Tokyo, Nov. 1943), pp. 63-65. Conveniently quoted in F. C. Jones, *Japan's New Order in East Asia* (New York: Oxford University Press, 1954), pp. 470-471.

stability of East Asia. Herein lies the cause of the present war.

The countries of East Asia, with a view to contributing to the cause of world peace, undertake to cooperate towards prosecuting the war of Greater East Asia to a successful conclusion, liberating their region from the yoke of British-American domination and assuring their self-existence and self-defence and in constructing a Greater East Asia in accordance with the following principles:—

I. The countries of Greater East Asia, through mutual cooperation will ensure the stability of their region and construct an order of common prosperity and well-being based upon justice.

II. The countries of Greater East Asia will ensure the fraternity of nations in their region, by respecting one another's sovereignty and independence and practising mutual assistance and amity.

III. The countries of Greater East Asia, by respecting one another's traditions and developing the creative faculties of each race, will enhance the culture and civilization of Greater East Asia.

IV. The countries of Greater East Asia will endeavor to accelerate their economic development through close cooperation upon a basis of reciprocity and to promote thereby the general reciprocity of their region.

V. The countries of Greater East Asia will cultivate friendly relations with all the countries of the world and work for the abolition of racial discrimination, the promotion of cultural intercourse, and the opening of resources throughout the world and contribute thereby to the progress of mankind.

— Reading No. 10 —

PANTJA-SILA—THE BASIC PHILOSOPHY OF THE INDONESIAN STATE, JUNE 1, 1945[1]

"Not under the full moon, but under the sound of the drums of war and in the fury of war," Sukarno expounded this distillation of his political thought to the "Committee to Investigate and Prepare Indonesian Independence."

✓ ✓ ✓

What is it that is called freedom? In 1933 I wrote a booklet called "Towards a Free and Independent Indonesia" where I stated that freedom was nothing more than a "bridge," a golden bridge, on the far side of which we were to rebuild our society. . . .

International law itself does not require any complicated, hairsplitting conditions for freedom and independence. The possession of a territory, a people, and a stable government is sufficient in international law. Whether the people can read or not, are rich or poor, clever or stupid, does not matter. If, in accordance with international law, the nation possesses the conditions for an independent state, viz. a people, a territory, and a government, it is independent.

Now that I have dealt with the question of Freedom,

[1] *Indonesian Review*, Vol. I, No. 1, January, 1951. Published by the Indonesia Publishing Institute "Prapanca," Kramat 99, Djakarta.

and Independence, I will proceed to deal with the question of principles. . . .

The First Principle, which is to be the foundation of our State of Indonesia, is the *principle of Nationalism*. . . .

Briefly speaking, the people of Indonesia, the Indonesian nation are not the group of individuals who, having *"le désir d'être ensemble,"* live in a small area like Minangkabau or Madura or Djokja or Pasundan or Makassar; no, the Indonesian people are those human beings who, according to God-ordained geo-politics, live throughout the entity of the entire archipelago of Indonesia from the northern tip of Sumatra to Papua! All, throughout the islands! Because amongst these seventy million human beings there exists already *"le désir d'être ensemble,"* the *"Charactergemeinschaft."* The Indonesian nation, the people of Indonesia, the Indonesian human beings which number seventy millions who have united to become one, and form one single entity. . . .

We must not only establish the State of Free Indonesia, but we should also aim at making one family out of all nations of the world. This is the Second Principle of my philosophy of State, the *Principle of Internationalism*. But when I say "internationalism," I do not mean cosmopolitanism, for this negates nationalism, denies the existence of such nations as Indonesia, Japan, Burma, England, America, and so on. Internationalism cannot flower if it is not rooted in the soil of nationalism. Nationalism cannot flower if it does not grow within the garden of internationalism. . . .

What is the Third Principle? This is the *Principle of Consent*, the *Principle of Representative Government*. We are to establish a State "all for all," "one for all, all for one," not a State for the benefit of one particular group, not a State for the wealthy. . . . Allah, God of the Universe, gave us the capacity to think, so that in our daliy intercourse we might constantly burnish our thoughts. Just as the pounding and husking of paddy results in our getting rice, our best food, argument and discussion in our daily intercourse results in the clarification of our thoughts.

The Fourth Principle I am proposing is the *Principle*

of Prosperity, the principle: that there be no poverty in free Indonesia. . . . The democracy we are seeking is not the democracy of the west, but a politico-economic democracy, which will result in the good life and social prosperity. . . . The people know what it is not to have enough to eat nor enough to wear, and now wish to create a new world of justice in accordance with the precepts of Ratu Adil. . . .

Thus, the people's assembly to be established must not be a body for the discussion of political democracy only, but a body which is to translate into reality the two principles: *Political Justice* and *Social Justice.* . . .

The Fifth Principle should be the recognition of the *Divine Omnipotence,* the organization of Free Indonesia on the basis of *Belief in God.* . . . The Christian should worship God according to the teachings of Jesus Christ. Moslems according to the teaching of the Prophet Mohammed, Buddhists should discharge their religious rites according to their own books. . . .

Hence, if the people of Indonesia desire that the Pantja Sila I propose become a reality . . . we must not forget the condition for its realization, viz. struggle, struggle, and once again, struggle! . . . If the people of Indonesia are not united, not determined to live or die for freedom, this freedom will never come to the Indonesian people, never, until the end of time. Freedom and independence can only be won and enjoyed by a people when the soul is aflame with the determination of "MERDEKA- FREEDOM or DEATH!"

— Reading No. 11 —

NEW CONCEPT OF GOVERNMENT STRUCTURE—PRESIDENT SUKARNO, FEBRUARY 21, 1957[1]

At eight o'clock in the evening of February 21, 1957, the people of Indonesia from Sabang to Merauke tuned their radios to President Sukarno's new plan to overcome the difficulties which plagued the suffering state. More than nine hundred guests—big and small captains of political parties and mass organizations which littered the Indonesian nation—gathered in the "Istana Negara" or state palace to hear the dramatic details of the New Concept. Indonesians and their friends hoped that the New Concept or the "Guided Democracy," as it was labelled abroad, would overcome the national emergency. Skeptics and critics—noting the overtones of dislike of parties, virtue of struggle, beauties of leadership, and the elimination of opposition—were haunted by echoes of prewar Germany, Italy, and Japan or feared the beginning of a new totalitarianism of the left.

✦   ✦   ✦

Brethren, I need not tell you that our state is in distress. . . . And the difficulties now confronting us are not of recent origin—they have been of long standing, but have only recently reached their climax. . . . Ever since we proclaimed the Republic of Indonesia on 17th

[1] "To Preserve the Republic We Have Proclaimed" (Concept of H. E. President Sukarno). Message delivered by H. E. President Sukarno in "Istana Negara" (state palace) on February 21, 1957. Mimeographed release. No specific date or place of publication.

August 1945, the Indonesian people, who formerly thought that the proclamation and the state would bring peace, happiness and joy, were for eleven years constantly —I nearly say "permanently"—disturbed. . . .

In my opinion, we should set up an altogether new system of government . . . We should not only pull down the pillars, the roof, the walls; we should pull down everything—not excluding the foundation—and lay a new foundation, erect a totally new building, that is, the new-style governmental structure of the Republic of Indonesia. . . .

The experiences of these eleven years have convinced me that the democracy we have adopted, the democracy we have used, is a democracy which is not in harmony with the soul of the Indonesian nation. . . . Brethren, in this Western . . . parliamentary democracy, we come across the idea of opposition. It is this very idea of opposition, brethren, which has made us go through hardships for eleven years. Because we interpret this idea of opposition in a manner which does not agree with the Indonesian soul. . . . It is clear that opposition is interpreted as downright criticism of the government, *coûte que coûte!* It is clear that opposition is interpreted as the endeavour to overturn the existing government, whenever possible, and its replacement by a government of the opposition itself.

What then is my Concept? My Concept consists of two items: the first concerns the Cabinet; the second concerns the National Council.

What about the Cabinet? As to the Cabinet, my brethren, we should form a *Gotong-Rojong* (Mutual Assistance) Cabinet. I expressly use the term *Gotong-Rojong,* because this is an authentic Indonesian term which gives the purest reflection of the Indonesian soul. The Cabinet should comprise all political parties and groups represented in Parliament which have attained a certain electoral quotient. . . . Parliament goes on. . . .

How then should the *Gotong-Rojong* Cabinet I propose be set up? I just said that we should not discriminate: that we should no longer ask: are you Masjumi, are you P.K.I., are you Nahdatul Ulama, are you Protestant, are you Catholic? No, we should not. All parties in Parliament should be given the right to participate in the Cabinet. So many members in Parliament, so many ministers in the Cabinet. This is just, my brethren. Just, because it does not discriminate; just, because we simply regard ourselves as—no more or less—Indonesians.

Next to the *"Gotong-Rojong"* Cabinet I propose . . . a National Council (which) shall include a representative of . . . labour circles, . . . the peasants . . . the intelligentsia, . . . the group of national entrepreneurs, . . . the Protestant group, . . . the Catholic group, . . . the "Alim Ulama" (Muslim theologians), . . . the women group, . . . the youth group, . . . the 1945 generation, . . . the group which can express or set forth the problems of the regions. And besides these, my brethren, I wish that the National Council shall also include the Chief of Staff of the Army, the Chief of Staff of the Navy, the Chief of Staff of the Air Force, the Chief of the State Police, the Attorney-General, several Ministers who hold important portfolios; and, my brethren, God willing, this National Council will be led by myself. . . .

— Reading No. 12 —

A YEAR OF DECISION (1957)— PRESIDENT SUKARNO [1]

On August 17, 1957, the twelfth anniversary of Indonesian independence, President Sukarno launched the "New Life Movement." He renewed his attack on imported democracy and denied that the New Life Movement received its inspiration from any outside source, particularly the Peoples Republic of China. He sought to expound a social philosophy for Indonesians to which

[1] Ministry of Information, Djakarta, 1957.

*the institutions of his Guided Democracy would be
dedicated.*

↑   ↑   ↑

Brethren and Sisters. . . . A kaleidoscope of good and
evil, the whole gamut of progress and recession, of patriotism and stupidity, has filled the Indonesian air these
last few years, and has lately disturbed the Indonesian
skies. . . .

In the course of twelve years, however, we have witnessed seventeen cabinet changes; a lot of bother over
regional affairs; a lot of bother in army circles; not the
right kind of industrialization but the patchwork kind,
without any proper over-all planning; we have not seen
food sufficiency but incessant rice imports. We have not
witnessed a soaring growth of national culture of which
we may be justly proud but—the madness of rock and
roll. We have not been witnesses to the melodiousness of
pure Indonesian music, but to the din of swing and jazz
and mambo rock. We have not been witnesses to the
creative power of excellent Indonesian literature but to a
flood of comics.

And all this because of decline in the sense of national
dignity, a decline in the pride and respect for the ability
and identity of our own nation and our own people!
Truly, the ability and identity of our own people! The
common people, the tens of millions of people, who like
ants earn their living, rear their offspring, laugh and cry,
live and die—the people whose countenances are reflective of the nation's strength and identity, who conduct is
reflective of the nation's tenacity and character. . . .

As I said at Bandjarmasin a few weeks ago, we are
suffering from talkativeness and from a misconcept of
democracy. . . . Indeed, it is obvious that the democracy
we have put into effect in Indonesia up to now is *not*
a system that is the best suited, and the most appropriate,
to the identity and the mental outlook of the Indonesian
people. . . . It has become apparent that democracy
without discipline and guidance has merely turned into a
chatterbox democracy, a democracy that is not capable
of giving birth to new and constructive ideas. It has become apparent that this sort of democracy has only given

birth to a society of political parties, where the upper classes only live parasitical lives.

There is not the least vestige left of our national dignity, so that a great many of us are not ashamed at seeing part of the outside world shaking its head, and another part showing malicious pleasure. They are not ashamed to hear the outside world say: "Indonesia is breaking up"—"Quo vadis Indonesia?"—"A nation in collapse." . . .

Therefore, it is necessary for us to make corrections in the political system we have been carrying into effect up to now—in the system we have bodily imitated from abroad. We must not apply free-fight liberalism, but a kind of democracy which contains the idea of *management* toward *one* aim, i.e.: *a society based on social justice*. A democracy that recognizes discipline; a democracy that is in keeping with the Indonesian nation's mental outlook, i.e. mutual help; a democracy that restricts itself to one aim; a democracy having a leadership; *a guided democracy*. . . .

Give our nation a democracy that does not run wild. . . . Because, a democracy that allows the group or the individual to have a thousand and one aims, will drown the national interests in the vortex of catastrophe! . . . Because, if not focussed on the state and on the nation, democracy will become a tool of political corruptors. Without honest members, democracy will become the dance hall of grandstand adventurers who do not recognize any moral but self-seeking. In the absence of persons with creative power, democracy will become the meeting place of people who are impotent to create anything whatsoever, the meeting place of old women who indulge in aimless debating. . . .

Brethren and sisters! . . . We are now in the second stage of our Revolution, i.e. the stage of nation-building. The first stage is the stage of breaking the shackles, the stage of liberation. In the first stage we burst the chains which fettered us for centuries; bamboo spears and guns, matchets and grenades, bombs and dynamite were our playthings. We rushed all the strongholds of imperialism, we smashed up all bulwarks of colonialism. How grievous was that time, but at the same time how glorious it was!

Our ambitions soared high our readiness to fight and sacrifice knew no bounds. Our spirit flamed and shone like a dancing fireball. Both the masses and the leaders wore jute clothes, but there was the glow of a sacred fire in their eyes, and there was a smile on their lips. Everything seemed easy of attainment. . . .

However, when we embarked upon nation-building, all kinds of eccentricities reared their heads. Water, when it is on its upper reaches of a river, rushes from one boulder to another, from one steep bank to another, and is always clear and pure. When it arrives in the lowlands it is no longer tempestuous, its flow has become quiet, and each of its eddies produces foam. . . .

Indeed, how many are the diseases which afflict us, which retard the progress of our nation-building . . . Why do not people arrive at their offices before nine o'clock, and why do they make preparations to go home as early as one o'clock? Why do we fall so completely for foreign luxury imports? Why do we not give sufficient thought to saving? Why are we so fond of extravagant luxury? Why have we lost our alertness and have become sluggish? Why is our labour efficiency not higher than 50 per cent? Why have a great many of us forgotten the ideals of our Independence Proclamation? . . . Why does it look as if we have lost our identity? Why has the sense of oneness and unity lost its former intensity? Why are there so many political adventurers? What has made the scum rise to the surface? Why are our railway trains so dirty, while the state has paid so much to buy them? What is the reason that we still go about with the stigma of "islander" on our foreheads? . . .

Let the bitter experience of the past serve as a warning, if we do not want to be a great ass. . . . The New Life Movement does not only mean an "austerity" movement. Mentally we must be completely rejuvenated, completely washed clean and completely scrubbed clean. Mentally we must be completely forged again. What is this austerity for, if it amounts to the scantiness of the pauper who lives on rice and salt; who does not eat off a plate but from a banana leaf; who sleeps on a worn-out mat; but whose soul is that of a living corpse, with not the slightest spark of life, gleam of idealism, will to fight.

What is such kind of austerity for?

That is not the kind of austerity we mean. The austerity we mean is the austerity of a soldier in battle whose spirit soars high, whose soul is full of creative power, whose ambition is as tempestuous as the ocean, whose soul is the soul of the Indonesian idealist—as if it were made up of starlight, which refuses to be static because the thunder and the lightning are its shining examples. The austerity of the soldier who has no need of gold and diamonds; of reputation and position; but wants to serve —to serve God, ideals, country, nation, society, and the unitary state.

Brethren and sisters, keep this in mind: This year is a year of decision. Shall we perish, or shall we survive? . . . We have come to a point of no return. There are only the alternatives: go back, stop, or go on. If we go back, we will be smashed up. If we stop, we will collapse. Therefore let us move on; let us leave the old things and enter into the new era. . . .

I repeat: the New Life Movement is not merely a movement to teach people that they may not spit at random; that they must not throw away their cigarette stubs on the floor. It is a movement for a Mental Revolution. It is a Movement to forge the Indonesian into a new man—pure-hearted, steel-willed, with the spirit of the Eagle and a soul of fire. . . . A nation that always wallows in the mire will be a gutter nation. A nation that has the spirit of a Radjawali will be with God. . . .

Bismillah! Let us now embark upon the New Life Movement.

— Reading No. 13 —

MERDEKA FOR THE FEDERATION OF MALAYA, 1957[1]

Merdeka—independence—came to Malaya in 1957. It was accomplished not by bloodshed but by peaceful agreement between the Malay States, the Settlements of Penang and Malacca, and the British sovereign. This reading is a series of pertinent quotations from the five major documents:

(A) The Federation of Malaya Agreement, August 5, 1957;

(B) The Proclamation of Independence, August 31, 1957;

(C) Speech by H.R.H. the Duke of Gloucester at the Independence of Malaya Celebrations on August 31, 1957;

(D) Speech at the Proclamation of Independence by Prime Minister of Malaya Tunku Abdul Rahman, August 31, 1957;

(E) Agreement between the United Kingdom and Malaya on External Defence and Mutual Assistance, October 12, 1957.

✦   ✦   ✦

(A) . . . . As from the thirty-first day of August, nineteen hundred and fifty-seven, the Malay States and the Settlements shall be formed into a new Federation of States by the name of Persekutuan Tanah Melayu, or in

[1] Released by the Federal government of Malaya, Department of Information on dates indicated. Text of Treaty on External Defence and Mutual Assistance published September 20, 1957.

134

English, the Federation of Malaya . . . and thereupon the said Settlements shall cease to form part of Her Majesty's dominions and Her Majesty shall cease to exercise any sovereignty over them, and all power and jurisdiction of Her Majesty or of the Parliament of the United Kingdom in or in respect of the Settlements or the Malay States or the Federation as a whole shall come to an end.

(B) . . . . AND WHEREAS by the Federal Constitution aforesaid provision is made to safeguard the rights and prerogatives of Their Highnesses the Rulers and the fundamental rights and liberties of the people and to provide for the peaceful and orderly advancement of the Persekutuan Tanah Melayu as a constitutional monarchy based on parliamentary democracy. . . .

Now in the name of God the Compassionate, the Merciful, I, TUNKU ABDUL RAHMAN PUTRA ibni AL-MABHUM SULTAN ABDUL HAMID HALIM-SHAH, PRIME MINISTER OF THE PERSEKUTUAN TANAH MELAYU, with the concurrence and approval of Their Highnesses the Rulers of the Malay States do hereby proclaim and declare on behalf of the people of the Persekutuan Tanah Melayu that as from the thirty-first day of August, nineteen hundred and fifty-seven, the Persekutuan Tanah Melayu . . . is and with God's blessing shall be forever a sovereign democratic and independent state founded upon the principles of liberty and justice and ever seeking the welfare and happiness of its people and the maintenance of a just peace among all nations.

(C) . . . (The Duke of Gloucester) It has been the aim and ambition both of Her Majesty's Government in London and of the officers of Her Majesty's Overseas Civil Service who have worked with and among you to help you to take your rightful place in the modern world. Malaya has now the highest standard of living in Southeast Asia; equal justice before the law, and freedom of worship for all religions are assured; and for the last nine years you have been gaining experience in the ideals and workings of democratic institutions. The preamble to the Agreement made in 1948 between my late Brother King George VI and Their Highnesses the Rulers contained this declaration: "It is the desire of His Majesty and

Their Highnesses that progress should be made towards eventual self-government." That goal has now been achieved and with it the independence we are today celebrating.

But this we believe is by no means the end of close and cordial relations between our two countries but the beginning of a new chapter. A jewel is beautiful in itself but far more beautiful when it is set and mounted in fine gold. Today not only does Malaya wear the jewel of independence but that jewel is mounted in the unrivalled setting of the Commonwealth. I know that Malaya will play an important and creative part in the unique association of free peoples and that in this setting the jewel of independence will shine with its greatest lustre. . . .

(D) . . . . (The Prime Minister of Malaya). We in Malaya have a long history, but we do not lightly forget old relationships. . . . We shall therefore always remember with gratitude the assistance which we have received from Great Britain down our long path to nationhood; an assistance which culminates today with the proclamation of Malaya's independence. . . . Malaya will henceforward take her place in the great Commonwealth of independent nations whose members are found in all parts of the world, and as an equal partner in that great association. . . .

(E) . . . ARTICLE VI. In the event of a threat of armed attack against any of the territories or forces of the Federation of Malaya or any of the territories or protectorates of the United Kingdom in the Far East or any of the forces of the United Kingdom with those territories or protectorates or within the Federation of Malaya, or other threat to the preservation of peace in the Far East, the Governments of the Federation of Malaya and of the United Kingdom will consult together on the measures to be taken jointly or separately to ensure the fullest cooperation between them for the purpose of meeting the situation effectively.

ARTICLE VII. In the event of an armed attack against any of the territories or forces of the Federation of Malaya or any of the territories or protectorates of the United Kingdom in the Far East or any of the forces of the United Kingdom within any of those territories or protectorates or within the Federation of Malaya, the governments of the Federation of Malaya and the United Kingdom undertake to cooperate with each other and will take such action as each considers necessary for the purpose of meeting the situation effectively.

— Reading No. 14 —

WHEN CHRISTIANITY MET BUDDHISM IN SIAM—ABOUT 1850[1]

For a long time, the labors of missionaries in Siam produced few converts. Buddhism by habit and education had become part of Siamese nature and would not bend to sectarian quarrels of foreign missionaries. King Mongkut told Mrs. Leonowens he hoped "you will do your best endeavor for knowledge of English language, science, and literature and not for conversion to Christianity." What follows is a faithful report of a conversation between one of the most distinguished nobles in Siam and a Christian Protestant missionary.

↑   ↑   ↑

Nobleman. After all, my religion is a better religion than yours.

Missionary. Convince me of that and Your Excellency shall be *my* teacher.

N. This is my religion: To be so little tied to the world that I can leave it without regret; to keep my heart sound; to live doing no injustice to any, but deeds of compassion to all.

M. This is excellent: this accords with my teaching; but will Your Excellency tell me what those must do who have already committed sin?

N. Why should they sin?

M. Who has not sinned: We should own we have

---

[1] Sir John Bowring, *The Kingdom and People of Siam* (London: John W. Parker and Son, 1857) 2 vols., I, 378 ff.

sinned; we Christians have One who has removed our sins from us, and taken them upon himself; but you——

N. Where have I sinned? I do not acknowledge sin.

M. But it is not enough that men should be honest and kind to one another. They owe allegiance to God, their great Sovereign. To disobey Him, to forget Him, to avoid His presence, to be indifferent to His favor—this is sin.

N. And so you think God is censorious and jealous of His creatures, and wants their services and their praises? No! Let us treat all men justly. God is absorbed, gone into annihilation. We need not be troubled or think about Him.

M. No! He lives above. He is *our* Master. It is not enough that servants should be honest towards their fellows, kind to their wives and children; they owe to *their* Master service and gratitude, and will be punished if they do not render them.

N. Who is to punish? You call sin what is no sin.

M. But does not Your Excellency flog your servants when they disobey? Do you pardon them solely because they have not wronged their fellow servants?

N. (*Much excited*). What service does God want of us? He is not envious and covetous, as you fancy Him to be.

M. Suppose I told Your Excellency's servants that nothing was required of them but to live honestly and pleasantly together; to care nothing about you—neither to seek to please, nor obey, nor serve you, nor be thankful for Your Excellency's kindness: will you allow this? . . .

N. Now I will tell you of your heavy sins.

M. Show it to me and I will confess.

N. Why don't you take a wife?—Why don't you provide successors to teach your religion when you are gone? Christ had thirty disciples, had he not? and his disciples had wives and children; and they multiplied, and have overrun the world; but your religion and your name would perish together if others followed your example.

M. Others will take care of this.

N. No! Each man has a duty for himself.

M. Your Excellency is right. I am beaten here; but your Buddhist priests enjoin celibacy.

N. Battle it then with the Buddhist priests and not with

me. . . . Now how long have you American missionaries been here?

M. Nineteen years.

N. Have you made a single convert?

M. Not among the Siamese; and we acknowledge our disappointment but are not discouraged. If a merchant sent out his agents and they failed, he would recall them; but those who sent us would think their sacrifices well repaid if a single soul were saved; for a soul is not extinguished by death, but lives forever; and we know that Siam will become a Christian country.

N. But the Siamese are not savages of the woods, having no religion and therefore ready to receive one. We have our religion, in which we have been brought up from our childhood; it will not easily be rooted out. Has it been in any single instance? The work would be difficult.

— Reading No. 15 —

KING MONGKUT'S PERSONAL LETTER TO PRESIDENT FRANKLIN PIERCE, MAY 31, 1856[1]

King Mongkut was proud as a peacock about his title "Professor of Pali Language and Buddhistic Literature" and his prowess with the English language. After he really opened Siam to the British in a treaty with the distinguished diplomat, Sir John Bowring, the king turned his attention to the waiting representative from the United States, Townsend Harris. He had received from the American minister plenipotentiary a personal letter from the President together with some modest gifts. The king acknowledged the compliments in the delightful but slightly complicated handwritten letter below.

✔   ✔   ✔

(King's Seal)

Manu Regi	The Sovereignty of
Siamensium	Siamese Kingdom
Anno Sixemo	and its
	Dependencies

Somdetch Phra Paramendr Maha Mongkut,

By the blessing of highest and greatest superagency of Universe,

The King of Siam and Sovereign of all tributary countries adjacent in every direction namely Laos, Sheangs,

[1] "English Correspondence of King Mongkut," in Journal of Siam Society, vol. XXI pt. I (Bangkok, 1927), p. 30.

Laokans, Cambodia, Kareungs and most of Malay Peninsula and professor of Pali language and Buddhistical literature, &c., &c.,

To all and singular to whom these presents shall come, Greeting!

We have acknowledged the receipt of the letter of the President of the United States of America, whose name is Franklin Pierce, dated City Washington, twelfth of September 1855, handed us by the Honble. Townsend Harris, Esquire, who is the envoy appointed to make a new treaty with us as amending the old treaty of the said country with ours for being improved and more advantageous to both sides in similar manner of that with English Government just done.

We have the said letter perused at our Supreme Court on the first day of May, 1856.

Agreeably to request of Government of United States of America, we have counsel of whole Royalty and our Council and appointed one of our royal brother, three high ministers officers of State who were totally four individuals, ever have been appointed Plenipotentiaries on our part and held the consultation and made the new treaty with Sir John Bowring, English Plenipotentiary on last year; and add the other one in place of our first Regent who had been one of the five plenipotentiaries in last year and lost his life in the time of the treaty with English was just sealed and signed on 18th April, 1855— so our plenipotentiaries were full five individuals invested with full power to make the new Treaty of Friendship and Commerce between Siam and the United States of America on our part and hold consultation with Townsend Harris, Esquire, the envoy plenipotentiary of U. S. of America. Their names and offices were fully mentioned in the form of the treaty.

Although they were appointed by us on very early part of the current month, but in consequence of their business in being our Royal Commissioners to make the agreement (which is a commentary of the treaty with English both old and new) with Mr. Harry Smith Parkes, who was bearer of ratifications of the new treaty from England for exchange here and prepare all its provisions, after this agreement was done on late of the present month, they have held the consultation with Townsend Harris, Esquire, on few occasions—the American envoy has framed the new treaty in a very similar manner of that of English and wrote in triplicate, which were concluded by signature of both Siamese and American plenipotentiaries on the 29th May, 1856.

After which date Townsend Harris, Esquire, was in greatest hurrying for his departure on 31st May. We could not postpone his departure for a few days more in next week. We regret very much we could not furnish proper royal letter in answer to the letter addressed us by the President of U. S. of America and already in picking and preparing the suitable royal presents for the President, who have goodness enough to offer us his good friendship remarked by his valued presents designed to us on this occasion, as the time is very narrow between the day of the conclusion of the treaty and departure of the envoy. Therefore for declaration our being sincerely gratitude to the President of the United States of America indeed and for our further promise that we send royal letter and suitable royal presents to America on other occasion by any rate when good opportunity allow. We wrote these present with our royal hand and sealed with Great Seal of our kingdom and our official and particular seals for our Royal Standard—to be a credentials from us in hand of Honble. Townsend Harris, Esquire, the envoy.

Given at our court of Amarindr Winechae Ratne Kasindr, Bangkok on the Saturday 12th, the Waning Moon in the Lunar month of Wesakh in the year of Quadruped Serpent bearing number of Siamese Astronomical Era 1218, corresponding to the 31st May, 1856, of Christian era, which is the sixth of our reign.

| Major Rex | (Signed) S.P.P.M. MONGKUT |
| Siamensium | The First King of Siam |

(Endorsed:—First King's letter to the President of the United States.)

(The presents were then listed. . . .)

— Reading No. 16 —

KING CHULALONGKORN'S ADMONITIONS TO THE HEIR APPARENT, MAY 23, 1893 AND JULY 8, 1893[1]

King Chulalongkorn—the little prince in Anna and the King of Siam—was the contemporary of the Meiji emperor in Japan. The personal qualities of the king accounted in large measure for the modernization program which he carried out during his long reign (1868-1910). He revealed his deepest sentiments in letters to his children. He had thirty-four sons and forty-three daughters. He put the best of his philosophy of kingship in letters to the first crown prince, Caofa Maha Vajirunhis, whom death deprived of his royal heritage.

✶   ✶   ✶

A king should devote himself above all to truth and honesty, he should never be prone to thoughts and acts of revenge or jealousy; he should bind the royal family and his statesmen in unity. . . .

When I became king at the age of fifteen, conditions were such that I seemed like a weak flickering flame that might go out at any moment. I stuck to honesty, never entertaining thoughts of revenge, trying to follow in the

[1] King Chulalongkorn, *Letters, Miscellaneous,* Part I. Published and dedicated to her sister the late Princess Prabha, on the occasion of the cremation of her remains by Her Royal Highness, Princess Vapi Bushakor, (Bangkok, 1950), pp. 15 ff. Excerpts quoted in Journal of Siam Society, vol. XXXVIII, pt. 2. (Bangkok, 1951), p. 92.

footsteps of my august predecessors and relying upon a vigilant care of my duties. . . .

At that time, I was fifteen years and ten days old, without a mother. None of my relatives on the maternal side were particularly able. As for my paternal relatives, that is to say the high princes, they were all under the influence of the Somdec Chao Phya and had to look to their personal safety and well-being rather than supporting me. Some of them just took no interest in the affairs of state. As for the officials, some, it is true, were devoted to me, but they were mostly junior ones. My own brothers and sisters, being minors could be of no help. As for myself, at that age I knew nothing of statecraft and was so seriously ill that but few people thought I would survive. At the time of my father's death, therefore I was like a human trunk, the head of which had just been cut off, propped up merely to serve as a figurehead. . . . The crown weighed heavily upon me. The lamp of my life was quickly extinguishing. But how did it not go out? . . . It was owing to these causes:

1. Medicine and non-indulgence, such as in rich food;

2. Determination to be fair to all . . .

3. An attitude of respect towards my senior relatives who kept aloof and sincerely believed at first that I was destined to be a mere figurehead, though they gradually took pity on me later;

4. The good will of officials who took a friendly liking for me perhaps in the hope that they might some day reap the reward of their loyalty thus offered to me;

5. My constant attitude of forgiveness and civility to that quarter which was known to be my enemy at heart;

6. My fair treatment of those officials who obviously sat on the fence awaiting the turn of events, to which attitude of theirs I just paid no attention;

7. My refrain from unduly favoring my own people in every way;

8. My sacrifice of personal comfort and luxury;

9. When I found that I could count upon more supporters, I began to expand my influence for good. Once people saw that I could succeed, more began to give me their cooperation and enemies relaxed their antagonism, some even turning to my side;

10. I do not deny having been at times involved in indiscreet acts of youth which landed me in difficult situations but my general behavior towards people and my fairness to all somehow saved such situations. . . .

You are having a better time than I. It is easier for you to be as good as I tried to be. . . .

Be generous and kind to your relatives and friends, particularly your half-brothers. . . . Be modest and show respect for your elders, whether they belong to the royal family or not. . . . Do not think that you are born to enjoy yourself, because you are born with a duty to work in order to receive merit. . . . Do not think that to be king is to be rich or to do whatever you want or to take revenge on anyone who has harmed you or to live well.

To live easily, first is to be a priest and second is to be rich. To be a king, there are duties to be performed. You must be restrained in love and conquer hatred, anger, flattery, and laziness. The result of your merit will appear when you die. You will leave a good name as preserver of the family and protector of the people. These are two principles which you must have in mind more than anything else. If you cannot keep them in mind, you cannot rule and take care of the country. . . . It is a blessing that you have everything to make you ready to acquire knowledge, behave well and follow the path of merit.

— Reading No. 17 —

BURMA UNDER THE JAPANESE, 1942-1945—THAKIN NU[1]

The personal reactions to the Japanese occupation on the part of political leaders such as Laurel and Recto in the Philippines, Ba Maw and Thakin Nu in Burma, or Sukarno and Hatta in Indonesia, afford deep insights into a tortured period of history. Thakin Nu is a sensitive writer as well as a knowledgeable politician. He published his account of Burma under the Japanese in 1954, while he was prime minister of his country.

In the three selections which follow, he describes how quickly the ecstasy of freedom vanished before the disillusionment of a new tyranny; how an invaded nation formulated a practical code of behavior towards its conqueror; and how an astute, courageous "puppet" often proved to be a thorn in the flesh of his would-be manipulator.

⚹ ⚹ ⚹

At last Burma was to be free. . . .

The whole air was breathing rumors. 'The Japanese are our great friends.' 'When a Japanese meets a Burman he greets him with our own war cry.' 'The Japanese will die for Burma's freedom.' 'A Burman prince is coming as a leader in the Japanese army.' They all firmly believed the messages scattered down from aeroplanes and broadcast on the wireless that the Japanese were coming to help Burma, and rumor had swollen a handful of hope until it overflowed the basket. Now they were off to welcome their great ally the Japanese, and although it was close

[1] Thakin Nu, *Burma under the Japanese* (New York: St. Martin's Press, 1954), pp. 20-21; 47-48; 84; and 89-90.

on noon under the scorching sun of Mandalay, the poor people were so keen to greet their great ally that they did not even notice the heat.

We met them again in the afternoon about four o'clock. They were no longer marching in a procession but limping along in clumps of three or four. Their faces were no longer joyful and exultant as in the morning, and they seemed quite shy of facing the people who had stayed at home. When they came up to us, we asked what had happened. One of them replied in a surly tone. 'Don't talk about it. We expected the Japanese commander to be very thankful for our bowls of rice, but all he did was to take his hand out of his trouser pocket and give us a hard slap in the face.' And then he suddenly broke out laughing.

And another man chipped in, 'Talk about rough treatment. After he had slapped our faces he made us drag logs and draw water; drag, draw; drag, draw. It almost broke our backs.' Then they all burst out laughing. . . . And I thought to myself whatever one may say, there is nothing much wrong with Burmans who can see the funny side of things even in the most unpleasant circumstances. And from that time onwards the news spread like wildfire from one village to another that the Japanese were a tough crowd.

One had to be pretty careful not to make any mistakes. . . .

Suppose you exchanged cigarettes or a few sweetmeats with a Japanese. He may come along by himself and say there are a few things he does not understand very clearly. Or he may bring a friend and introduce him. One of them may remark that the Kempeitai, or the Japanese soldiers and traders, are a bad lot. You may be inclined to think that this Japanese is rather a decent sort. But don't go blurting out what you really think. For when you have met these men, you have not done with them. Suppose that the Japanese suspect you are a Communist. Some Japanese who say they are Communists will call on you. And they will fish for what they can find out. Someone will say that his younger brother has been arrested as a Communist. And they will tell you how badly the Japanese treat the Communists, giving them no more than a handful of rice and a cup of water a day, and how the government oppresses them. Or one of them will say that Communist ideas are very sound and that communism works to help the poor; that even the Japanese government has taken over many ideas from communism. So they tempt you with leading questions like digging a canal for water to run along.

And when you are looking at their stolid round faces, my friend, don't go thinking you are clever enough to deceive them. 'Least said, soonest mended.' There is always a chance of making a slip, and, even if what you have actually said may be all right, you may get into trouble because of some mistake by the interpreter, and everything that you say to the interpreter or the reporter or to that friend of yours or to the communists is reported to the police station. And any scrap of conversation with a Japanese spy who scrapes up acquaintance with you in the street or in the club or theater or market or opium den is reported to the police station. And the officer in charge compares it with all the other reports to check what you have said.

But they only take all these precautions, my friend, if you are an official of some standing. They don't take so much trouble to make up their mind about an ordinary man. A cup of boiling water, stripping the nails off three or four fingers, or a couple of turns with the machine round your testicles, and you will be ready to admit anything, true or false, in accordance with what they think.

So from the 1st of August (1943) I became the Minister of Foreign Affairs. . . . So far as possible I avoided the Japanese. . . . During the year that I was working in the Foreign Office there were only these three matters of any importance: apologizing for the Burman soldier; negotiating for the arrest of the Burman accused in the plot against the Adipati (leader); and arranging precedence at the wedding (of Dr. Ba Maw's daughter). Otherwise there was nothing worth mentioning. . . .

— Reading No. 18 —

PRIME MINISTER U NU OF BURMA SPEAKS ABOUT NEUTRALITY, JULY 1, 1955[1]

This speech, delivered to the National Press Club in Washington, D. C. is a clear, forceful exposition of the logic behind the philosophy and policy of "neutralism."

❧   ❧   ❧

. . . For a little over seven years now Burma has been a sovereign, independent nation. We are independent of foreign rule. And we are independent of any power blocs based on military treaties. Nations that choose not to participate in military blocs usually are referred to in this country as neutrals. If my impression is correct, this word "neutral" has acquired a distinct and unfavorable semantic coloration. Apparently, the word suggests the image of the ostrich with his head in the sand, a negative attitude towards world politics, a blind withdrawal from reality. The implication seems to be that a nation that does not choose sides and join irrevocably with one or the other camp in the armed truce that exists in the world today lacks courage and conviction. And very often the inference which seems to be drawn is "if you are not with us, then you are against us. And if you are not with us, you must be either openly or secretly in tow with communism." . . .

And if this is the case, there is real need for clarifica-

[1] *An Asian Speaks,* A Collection of Speeches made by U Nu, Prime Minister of Burma, during a visit to the United States of America June 29-July 16, 1955. Embassy of the Union of Burma, Washington, D. C., p. 13.

tion so that we can better understand each other. . . .

First of all, as most of you probably know, Burma has a long history. We had a great and flourishing civilization in Burma based on one of the great religions of the world, Buddhism, at the time when William the Conqueror was crossing the English Channel. This civilization, passed on to us by our forbears, has now become our national heritage. It is our way of life. We prefer it to any other way of life on this earth. We do not say that it cannot be improved, or that it cannot be adapted to suit modern conditions, but we do not wish to change its basis. We are not prepared to exchange it for any other way of life. This is not a matter of conceit. We do not claim that our way of life is better than that of other people. We merely say that it is different, that it suits us better, and that we therefore cannot be induced to give it up in exchange for some other way of life, be that the Communist way, the West European way, the American way, or any other way.

Now, I submit to you that if the citizens of any nation are deeply devoted to their culture, to their religion, to their way of life, to their country—as we in Burma are— then they will defend their way of life and their national frontiers with all the forces at their command. I can assure you that we are just as determined as any people to defend ourselves against foreign invasion or the imposition of any alien way of life by whatever method. And we have concluded that in the present phase of our history, and the present state of the world, the wisest, and even the only course for Burma is to pursue an independent policy, unshackled by what George Washington called "entangling foreign alliances."

Now I can hear some of you saying to yourselves, "How can he be so foolish? Burma is small; Burma is weak; how can she hope to repel foreign invasion alone? Besides, don't these Burmese know that the real danger to countries like Burma comes not from overt aggression, but from subversion? Surely their own interests demand that they should join in some military bloc which will give them the protection they need."

I am afraid I must beg to differ. To begin with, Burma is not alone. She is a member of the United Nations. As such she is entitled to the protection which collective security affords. The Charter of the United Nations is in effect one great mutual security pact. This is a fact which is often overlooked. . . .

It will probably be said at once that this implicit faith in the United Nations is pathetic; that the United Nations' system of collective security has broken down and can no longer be relied upon. Here again we must beg to differ. We say that the system has not broken down, but merely that it has not been made to work; that the remedy is not to push the United Nations aside but to strengthen it and put more life into it.

It is possible to disagree with this point of view. But whether one agrees or disagrees is immaterial, because in the present circumstances of Burma, her membership in any alliance with a great-power military bloc is incompatible with her continued existence as an independent state. This may seem to be putting it strongly, but it is a fact. Our recent history is such, our experience with great powers is such, that in the minds of the people of Burma an alliance with a big power immediately means domination by that power. It means the loss of independence. You may question the validity of that belief. But perhaps you will accept my statement that it is a political fact of life today that any government of Burma which aligned itself with a big-power bloc would at once lose the confidence and support of the people. In other words, the chances of subversion would be greatly increased. And if it is true that the real danger to countries like Burma lies in subversion rather than overt aggression, then it follows that membership in a big-power bloc would only tend to add to what is already said to be the greater of two dangers. . . .

In this talk, I have been trying to explain how our love of independence—call it preoccupation if you will—leads us logically and inevitably to the foreign policy of independence from any alignment of major powers on the basis of a military treaty. This policy has been called neutralism in the cold war. Perhaps that is the right name for it.

But I should like to take just another minute or two to point out that this is not a negative policy towards world affairs. Rather, it is a positive concept. It is a positive policy of seeking peace and friendship with all countries. It is a policy of actively seeking to discover through negotiation and compromise and accommodation some acceptable basis on which the peace of the world can be secured. Of course we do not pretend to have ready answers to these baffling and stubborn problems. But we do have the will to work actively, in collaboration with all, in searching for the answers. In the last analysis, the best way for a nation to promote its own security is to promote the peace. And we could not even hope to help promote the peace if we became members of an armed bloc. As independents, perhaps we can, and in doing so we would of course be serving the cause of democracy and the cause of man himself.

— Reading No. 19 —

DECLARATION OF INDEPENDENCE OF THE REPUBLIC OF VIETNAM, SEPTEMBER 2, 1945[1]

In the turmoil which followed the surrender of Japan in Southeast Asia, new nations were born. In exuberance of spirit, one of those nations—Vietnam—declared itself free and independent of France. Its words and sentiments recall the American document of 1776, even though the signature on the Vietnamese declaration is that of "President Ho-Chi-Minh."

✓　　　　✓　　　　✓

"All men are created equal. They are endowed by their Creator with certain inalienable rights, among these are Life, Liberty, and the Pursuit of Happiness."

This immortal statement was made in the Declaration of Independence of the United States of America in 1776. . . . The Declaration of the Rights of Man and the Citizen of the French Revolution in 1791 also states: "All men are born free and with equal rights, and must always be free and have equal rights." . . .

Nevertheless for more than eighty years, the French imperialists deceitfully raising the standard of Liberty, Equality, and Fraternity, have violated our fatherland and

[1] Government of Democratic Republic of Vietnam, *Documents* (no specific place or date of publication). Quoted in Allan B. Cole, *Conflict in Indo-China and International Repercussions, A Documentary History, 1945-1955* (Ithica: Cornell University Press, 1956), pp. 19-21.

oppressed our fellow citizens. They have acted contrarily to the ideals of humanity and justice.

In the province of politics, they have deprived our people of every liberty.

They have enforced inhuman laws; to ruin our unity and national consciousness, they have carried out three different policies in the north, the center and the south of Viet-nam.

They have founded more prisons than schools. They have mercilessly slain our patriots; they have deluged our revolutionary areas with innocent blood. They have fettered public opinion; they have promoted illiteracy.

To weaken our race they have forced us to use their manufactured opium and alcohol.

In the province of economics, they have stripped our fellow citizens of everything they possessed, impoverishing the individual and devastating the land.

They have robbed us of our rice fields, our mines, our forests, our raw materials. They have monopolized the printing of banknotes, the import and export trade; they have invented numbers of unlawful taxes, reducing our people, especially our country folk, to a state of extreme poverty.

They have stood in the way of our businessmen and stifled all their undertakings; they have extorted our working classes in a most savage way.

In the autumn of the year 1940, when the Japanese fascists violated Indochina's territory to get one more foothold in their fight against the Allies, the French imperialists fell on their knees and surrendered, handing over our country to the Japanese, adding Japanese fetters to the French ones. From that day on, the Vietnamese people suffered hardships yet unknown in the history of mankind. The result of this double oppression was terrific: from Quangtri to the northern border two million people were starved to death in the early months of 1945.

On the 9th of March, 1945, the French troops were disarmed by the Japanese. Once more the French either fled, or surrendered unconditionally, showing thus that not only were they incapable of "protecting" us, but that they twice sold us to the Japanese.

Yet, many times before the month of March, the Vietminh had urged the French to ally with them against the Japanese. The French colonists never answered. On the contrary, they intensified their terrorizing policy. Before taking to flight, they even killed a great number of our patriots who had been imprisoned at Yenbay and Cao-bang.

Nevertheless, towards the French people our fellow citizens have always manifested an attitude pervaded with toleration and humanity. Even after the Japanese putsch of March, 1945, the Vietminh have helped many Frenchmen to reach the frontier, have delivered some of them from Japanese jails, and never failed to protect their lives and properties. . . .

The whole population of Vietnam is united in common allegiance to the republican government and is linked by a common will, which is to annihilate the dark aims of the French imperialists.

We are convinced that the Allied nations which have acknowledged at Teheran and San Francisco the principles of self-determination and equality of status will not refuse to acknowledge the independence of Vietnam.

A people that has courageously opposed French domination for more than eighty years, a people that has fought by the Allies' side these last years against the fascists, such a people must be free, such a people must be independent.

For these reasons, we, members of the provisional government of Vietnam, declare to the world that Vietnam has the right to be free and independent, and has in fact become a free and independent country. We also declare that the Vietnamese people are determined to make the heaviest sacrifices to maintain its independence and its liberty.

FINAL DECLARATION OF THE GENEVA CONFERENCE ON THE PROBLEM OF RESTORING PEACE IN INDOCHINA, JULY 21, 1954[1]

Delegates from Cambodia, the Democratic Republic of Vietnam, France, Laos, the People's Republic of China, the State of Vietnam, the Union of Soviet Socialist Republics, the United Kingdom, and the United States met in Geneva and worked out armistice settlements for Cambodia, Laos, and Vietnam. Vietnam was divided—after the manner of Korea—into two zones at the seventeenth parallel. Three states—Cambodia, France, and Laos— issued statements of policy at the conference which are substantially repeated in the final declaration. Neither the United States nor the State of Vietnam (South Vietnam) accepted the declaration. The Geneva Settlement marked the end of the fighting phase in Indochina, but it by no means established an adequate basis for permanent peace.

✐   ✐   ✐

1. The Conference takes note of the agreements ending hostilities in Cambodia, Laos, and Vietnam and organising international control and the supervision of the execution of the provisions of these agreements.

2. The Conference expresses satisfaction at the ending

[1] Great Britain, *Further Documents relating to the Discussion of Indo-China at the Geneva Conference,* June 16-July 21, 1954. Miscellaneous No. 20 (1954), Cmd 9239, pp. 9-11 (London, 1954).

of hostilities in Cambodia, Laos, and Vietnam; the Conference expresses its conviction that the execution of the provisions set out in the present declaration and in the agreements on the cessation of hostilities will permit Cambodia, Laos, and Vietnam henceforth to play their part, in full independence and sovereignty, in the peaceful community of nations.

3. The Conference takes note of the declarations made by the Governments of Cambodia and Laos of their intention to adopt measures permitting all citizens to take their place in the national community, in particular by participating in the next general elections, which, in conformity with the constitution of each of these countries, shall take place in the course of the year 1955, by secret ballot and in conditions of respect for fundamental freedoms.

4. The Conference takes note of the clauses in the agreement on the cessation of hostilities in Vietnam prohibiting the introduction into Vietnam of foreign troops and military personnel as well as of all kinds of arms and munitions. . . .

5. The Conference takes note of the clauses in the agreement on the cessation of hostilities in Vietnam to the effect that no military base under the control of a foreign state may be established in the regrouping zones of the two parties, the latter having the obligation to see that the zones allotted to them shall not constitute part of any military alliance and shall not be utilized for the resumption of hostilities or in the service of an aggressive policy. . . .

6. The Conference recognizes that the essential purpose of the agreement relating to Vietnam is to settle military questions with a view to ending hostilities and that the military demarcation line is provisional and should not in any way be interpreted as constituting a political or territorial boundary. The Conference expresses its conviction that the execution of the provisions set out in the present declaration and in the agreement for the cessation of hostilities creates the necessary basis for the achievement in the near future of a political settlement in Vietnam.

7. The Conference declares that, so far as Vietnam is concerned, the settlement of political problems, effected on the basis of respect for the principles of independence, unity, and territorial integrity, shall permit the Vietnamese people to enjoy the fundamental freedoms, guaranteed by democratic institutions established as a result of free general elections by secret ballot. . . .

8. The provisions of the agreements on the cessation of hostilities intended to ensure the protection of individuals and of property must be most strictly applied and must, in particular, allow everyone in Vietnam to decide freely in which zone he wishes to live.

9. The competent representative authorities of the Northern and Southern zones of Vietnam, as well as the authorities of Laos and Cambodia, must not permit any individual or collective reprisals against persons who have collaborated in any way with one of the parties during the war, or against members of such persons' families.

10. The Conference takes note of the declaration of the government of the French Republic to the effect that it is ready to withdraw its troops from the territory of Cambodia, Laos, and Vietnam, at the request of the governments concerned and within periods which shall be fixed by agreement between the parties except in cases where, by agreement between the two parties, a certain number of French troops shall remain at specified points and for a specified time.

11. The Conference takes note of the declaration of the French government to the effect that for the settlement of all problems connected with the re-establishment and consolidation of peace in Cambodia, Laos, and Vietnam, the French government will proceed from the principle of respect for the independence and sovereignty, unity and territorial integrity of Cambodia, Laos, and Vietnam.

12. In their relations with Cambodia, Laos, and Vietnam, each member of the Geneva Conference undertakes to respect the sovereignty, the independence, the unity, and territorial integrity of the above-mentioned states, and to refrain from any interference in their internal affairs.

13. The members of the Conference agree to consult one another on any question which may be referred to

them by International Supervisory Commission, in order to study such measures as may prove necessary to ensure that the agreements on the cessation of hostilities in Cambodia, Laos, and Vietnam are respected. . . .

— Reading No. 21 —

VIETNAMESE DECLARATION AT THE GENEVA CONFERENCE, JULY 21, 1954[1]

The Vietnamese delegation refused to associate itself with the final declaration and placed on the record the following protest.

✓   ✓   ✓

"The delegation of the State of Vietnam has put forward its proposals aimed at obtaining an armistice without partition, even temporary, of Vietnam, by means of their disarmament of all the belligerent forces after their withdrawal into assembly areas as restricted as possible, and by the establishment of temporary control by the United Nations Organization over the whole of the territory until such time as the restoration of order and peace permits the Vietnamese people to decide its future by free elections.

The Vietnamese delegation protests against the rejection without examination of this proposal, which alone respects the aspirations of the Vietnamese people. It insists that the demilitarisation and neutralisation of the bishoprics of the Delta in North Vietnam should at least be accepted by the Conference. It protests solemnly against the hasty conclusion of the armistice agreement by the French and Viet Minh High Commands alone, in view of the fact that the French High Command only commands Vietnamese troops by delegation of the powers of

[1] Secretariat of State for Foreign Affairs, *Vietnam in World Affairs* (Saigon, 1956), vol. 1, nos. 1-11, p. 75.

the Chief of State of Vietnam, and above all in view of the fact that several clauses of this agreement are of a nature to compromise gravely the political future of the Vietnamese people.

The delegation protests solemnly that this armistice agreement abandons land to the Viet Minh, some of which are still occupied by Vietnamese troops, yet which are essential to the defence of Vietnam against further Communist expansion, which practically amounts to taking away from the State of Vietnam its inalienable right to organise its own defence in some way other than by maintaining a foreign army on its soil.

The delegation makes solemn protest against the fact that the French High Command has arrogated to itself the right, without prior agreement from the delegation of the State of Vietnam, to fix the date of future elections despite the clearly political character of such a provision.

Consequently, the government of the State of Vietnam demands that it should be put on record that it protests solemnly against the way in which the armistice was concluded and against the conditions of the armistice, which takes no account of the profound aspirations of the Vietnamese people, and that it reserves complete freedom of action for safeguarding the sacred right of the Vietnamese people to territorial unity, independence, and freedom.

— Reading No. 22 —

DECLARATION OF THE UNITED STATES ON GENEVA AGREEMENTS, JULY 21, 1954[1]

The government of the United States too could not accept the Geneva agreements, but it signified its intention not to disturb them by force.

✓ ✓ ✓

The Government of the United States, being resolved to devote its efforts to the strengthening of peace in accordance with the principles and purposes of the United Nations, takes note of the agreements concluded at Geneva declares with regard to the aforesaid agreements and paragraphs that (i) it will refrain from the threat or the use of force to disturb them . . . and (ii) it would view any renewal of aggression in violation of the aforesaid agreements with grave concern and as seriously threatening international peace and security.

In connection with the statement in the declaration concerning free elections in Vietnam, my Government wishes to make clear its position which it expresses in a declaration made in Washington on June 29, 1954, as follows:

'In the case of nations now divided against their will, we shall continue to seek to achieve unity through free elections supervised by the United Nations to insure that they are conducted fairly.'

With respect to the statement made by the representa-

[1] Department of State *Bulletin*, vol. XXXI, no. 788, August 2, 2, 1954, pp. 162, 163.

tive of the State of Vietnam, the United States reiterates its traditional position that peoples are entitled to determine their own future and that it will not join in any arrangement which would hinder this. Nothing in its declaration just made is intended to, or does, indicate any departure from this traditional position.

We share the hope that the agreements will permit Cambodia, Laos, and Vietnam to play their part in full independence and sovereignty, in the peaceful community of nations, and will enable the peoples of that area to determine their own future.

— Reading No. 23 —

PRESIDENT HO CHI MINH'S NATIONAL DAY SPEECH, SEPTEMBER 2, 1957[1]

North Vietnam is entirely different from the other countries of Southeast Asia in the nature of its values and its points of view. This document is intended to show the reasoning and the propaganda phrases employed behind the "bamboo curtain" in Asia. The quotations represent slightly less than half of the speech of President Ho Chi Minh delivered to a mass meeting in Hanoi in celebration of the twelfth anniversary of the founding of the Democratic Republic of Vietnam.

✦   ✦   ✦

Dear compatriots. . . .

During the past three years, our people in the north have made great efforts to overcome difficulties and to carry out production through labor. They have recorded great successes in healing the wounds of war, restoring economy, and starting the development of culture, thereby lessening difficulties in the life of the popular masses and gradually improving their living standards, in the delta regions as well as in the mountainous areas. Land reform has fundamentally been completed, the correction of errors committed and the work of developing the success obtained during that reform have been fruitfully carried out in many localities. Agriculture has visibly surpassed the prewar level. In industry, old factories have been

---

[1] *Vietnam Information Bulletin,* issued by the News Service of the Vietnam Democratic Republic, Rangoon, September 25, 1957, no. 38, 1957.

restored and new ones built. Order and security have been ensured and national defence strengthened. On behalf of the Party and Government, I congratulate the personnel of branches at all levels for their ardour in serving the people and in building up the fatherland.

Our task for this year is to further increase production and the practice of economy, to strive to fulfill the State Plan, to restore basically North Vietnam's economy, thereby progressively improve the living conditions of our people, and prepare conditions for us to advance in 1958 toward building the north under a long-term plan.

While the north of our country is becoming stronger and stronger, in the south, the American imperialists are intensifying their intervention, increasing their military personnel, catching hold of the South Vietnam economy. Together with the southern authorities, they have been sabotaging the Geneva agreements and the peace and unity of our country. They have resorted to all means of terror and repression with the aim of quenching the patriotism and the will for reunification of our southern compatriots. However the latter, always heroic, have unceasingly broadened their solidarity and struggle for the improvement of their standard of living, for democratic liberties, and for the peaceful reunification of their fatherland. Our government has recently proposed once again to the southern authorities contacts between the two zones and the re-establishment of normal north-south relations with a view to reaching a consultative conference on general elections to reunify the country. However, the southern authorities have obdurately persisted in their refusal, thus going counter to the deep aspirations of the entire people. . . .

I am now giving you a brief account of our visit to the brotherly countries. . . . I visited Korea, Czechoslovakia, Poland, the German Democratic Republic, Hungary, Yugoslavia, Albania, Bulgaria, and Rumania. On our way back and forth we stopped over for a few days in the Soviet Union and China. . . .

Everywhere from big towns to localities hundreds of kilometers from the capital cities, the peoples of brotherly countries welcomed us very warmly. At the great enthusiasm shown by the workers, peasants, intellectuals, and children, by young and old, we have vividly felt the sentiments of profound solidarity and friendship of the peoples of brotherly countries toward our people. This is not an honour peculiarly reserved for us, but a common honor for our people, for our Vietnamese fatherland. It is a manifestation of the lofty spirit of proletarian internationalism, a solid basis for lasting relations between brotherly countries of our great socialist family. . . .

We are happy to note that the building of socialism in brotherly countries is developing very rapidly. We have all realized what is the rhythm of economic development of our brotherly countries. It was only on the spot that we were able to realize the gigantic work of creative labor. One thing is very clear: numerous towns and capital cities such as Pyongyang, Warsaw, and Berlin, which were completely destroyed by the enemy during the war, have been rebuilt with great splendour. . . .

I am also very happy to inform you that in visiting our sisterly Hungary, we have noticed the marked elation of the Hungarian people, the return to normal life with factories, mines and farms, resuming their enthusiastic emulation in production as before. This is a great success of the brotherly Hungarian people, and also a great success for all of us. . . .

As regards the international situation we entirely agreed on the necessity to struggle for the defense of a lasting peace, and for the settlement of all international problems through peaceful negotiations; on the necessity to struggle for the materialization of the principles of peaceful coexistence, disarmament, the setting up of systems of collective security in Europe and Asia, and a ban on the use of atomic and hydrogen bombs. On our way back, during our stopover in Moscow, we learned that the Soviet Union had tested, with brilliant success an intercontinental rocket. This important event will have a sure effect on the defense of peace and will give more incentive to the struggle against the armament race and for disarmament. . . .

In short, between our country and fraternal countries, complete unity of views has been reached on all subjects discussed. This because we belong to the great socialist family and are all struggling under the glorious banner of Marxism-Leninism for the same lofty ideal which is Socialism. As our Solidarity and unity are strengthening day by day and no force can shake them, we will certainly be victorious. It may be said that our visit has been crowned with success, that it helped strengthen further the bonds of solidarity among the fraternal countries and raise still higher Vietnam's international position. On this occasion we would like to express once again our sincere thanks to all fraternal countries.

Dear compatriots. . . .

Our recent visit to fraternal countries lasted fifty-five days. It covered, there and back, nearly forty thousand kilometers, that is almost a tour of the globe. However, we had not the least impression of being foreigners. On the contrary, we felt ourselves at home among comrades, among people of the same heart, because socialist countries like ours are united like brothers of the same family. Is not that a proof that the great socialist family is great and mighty? Vietnam has the right to pride itself on belonging to this glorious and great family. . . .

Long live Vietnam peaceful, united, independent, democratic, prosperous, and strong!

Long live unity within the great family of socialist countries headed by the Soviet Union and China!

Long live friendship between the peoples of peace-loving countries of the world!

Long live world peace!

— Reading No. 24 —

PRESIDENT NGO DINH DIEM'S SPEECH ON THIRD ANNIVERSARY OF ACCESSION TO OFFICE; JULY 7, 1957[1]

On October 26, 1956 Premier Ngo Dinh Diem became president of Vietnam. The shift in title signified no transfer of power or responsibility. President Diem's administration of public affairs was continuous after July 7, 1954. After three years at the helm, he gave his people—and the world—the account of his stewardship which follows.

✓   ✓   ✓

Dear compatriots. . . .

Three years of struggle, three years of relentless efforts of the whole people from all walks of life, have brought the nation from a state of chaos and insecurity to the present peaceful and stable situation of a republic fully independent and endowed with democratic institutions and a democratic constitution. Internally the restoration of security has made possible the erection of a new political and economic structure. Externally, we have dashed the imperialists' dream of aggression, particularly that of the Communists' imperialism, extended friendly relations with countries of the free world, and enhanced Vietnam's prestige abroad.

First of all, national sovereignty has been wrest from

[1] Vietnam, *Authorized Translation of the President of the Republic's Message on Double Seven Day,* Saigon. July 10, 1957 is the date of the translation.

the hands of colonial and feudal forces, making possible the establishment of a republican regime based on the philosophy of personalism. . . .

Our success is due to the choice of a correct policy based on the social conditions of Vietnam, in accord with the people's aspirations and with human progress . . . In fact, to liberate the people in order to liberate the individual, it was necessary to know who oppressed, exploited, and trampled on the human dignity of the Vietnamese people. They are the colonialists, the feudalists, and the Communists . . .

Our compatriots must also realize fully that a complete change of regime, a revolution has taken place, not a common and simple struggle . . . In practice we have met many difficulties and obstacles:

There is no heavy industry in Free Vietnam, whose main resources are farm and forest products, and whose economy, trade, and finances are under the control of foreigners; long years of war have damaged seriously the communication system and rendered many people homeless; Vietnamese capital is insufficient and technicians are in short supply.

We have temporarily accepted aid from friendly countries, out of necessity and only temporarily . . .

I wish to stress the movement for rural community development.

This movement launched on March 1, 1957 has been enthusiastically welcomed by the people who have voluntarily contributed manpower and money and, under the guidance of government officials, have completed many projects of utility to the rural communities. . . .

I shall now give some figures to demonstrate the development of our national economy.

Agriculture.—In this field, the area of rice cultivated has been raised from 1,659,000 hectares in 1954 to 2,625,361 hectares in 1957 (i.e. a 58 per cent increase), that of fruit trees from 18,770 hectares to 26,274 hectares (i.e. a 30 per cent increase).

The 1956-1957 rice crop has yielded 3,514,621 metric tons compared with the 1955-1956 crop which produced only 2,816,670 tons. We are planning to export 300,000 tons of rice this year. Of this tonnage, a half was already exported. . . .

Land Reform.—The reduction of land rent and measures that conciliate the interests of the landowners and tenants have materialised, as is shown by the following facts:

—over 600,000 land-lease contracts were signed between landowners and tenants;

—farmers and cooperatives were granted loans totalling 250,000,000 piasters;

—26,120 hectares of lands were allotted to tenants who desired to become landowners (700 hectares are scheduled to be allotted to interested people). . . .

Commerce and Industry.—In the past three years, we have stabilized the market, regularized prices and assured economic rights for the Vietnamese.

Our people are now participating efficiently, in the field of domestic and foreign trade, industrial production, and handicrafts.

Over 750,000,000 piasters in loans were made available by the government for the benefit of our businessmen. In 1956 only local tradesmen and industrialists were granted government loans totalling 78,000,000 piasters. From July, 1956 to date, local products worth approximately 2.5 billion piasters have been exported.

Within the framework of the economic development program, the republican government has ordered the repair of over 2,800 kilometers of main highways alone, and more than 3,000,000 cubic meters of earth dredged from the waterways. . . .

From 1954 to 1957, the total enrollment in elementary schools has risen from 477,581 to 717,298; that of high schools from 47,890 to 72,020 (i.e. a 50 per cent increase). The number of students in technical schools has risen from 4,519 to 7,319 (a 61 per cent increase); that of students of universities from 2,109 to 3,823 (an 81 per cent increase). In the meantime, the number of adult literacy courses and night classes has greatly increased, thanks to the collaboration of various civic organizations. . . .

In this period, we shall seek to preserve and develop

the republican regime, increase national income, improve the people's living standard, and build up an independent and sound economy to liberate the individual.

Our efforts toward democracy both economically and socially will be the source of inspiration for our northern compatriots in their struggle to free North Vietnam from the Communist yoke.

This revolution and national reconstruction calls for relentless efforts from one and all of us. The higher one's position, the greater one's responsibilities. Soldiers, civil servants, and cadres as well as different organizations should strive to set good example to their fellow countrymen. . . .

The work of national reconstruction, of improvement of the people's living standard, and the achievement of an independent economy will be successfully achieved through the will, intelligence, and labor of the entire people; and we can surely achieve it.

— Reading No. 25 —

ROOTS OF PHILIPPINE POLICY— PRESIDENT RAMON MAGSAYSAY, 1956[1]

This article reflects not only the personal thoughts of the late, great president of the Philippines, but also the basic philosophy of the majority party—the Nacionalistas —whose platform was independence, but candidly in harmony with contemporary American views on foreign affairs. This philosophy, which at the time of writing was accepted by most Filipinos, explains the Philippine's readiness to join the Southeast Asia Collective Defense Organization and to champion the cause of the democracies or the free world publicly in propaganda fashion or privately in multilateral international gatherings.

✓   ✓   ✓

In shaping its foreign policy the Philippines is primarily moved by three considerations: . . . first, the strengthening of our national security by suppressing subversion from within and building strength against attacks from without through participation in collective security arrangements with other free nations; second, the utilization of the machinery of our foreign relations for the promotion of our foreign trade and economic cooperation in order to strengthen our domestic economy and to contribute our share to the economic development of a free world; and third, the development of our political and cultural relations with countries of the free world with particular emphasis on our relations with our Asian

[1] Ramon Magsaysay, "Roots of Philippine Policy," in *Foreign Affairs,* vol. 35, no. 1, October, 1956, pp. 29-36 (New York: Council on Foreign Relations, Inc.).

neighbors through our membership in the United Nations and by participation in regional conferences, such as the Manila Conference of 1954 (SEATO) and the Asian-African Conference in Bandung (1955).

In the pursuit of our objectives and in the choice of our methods our government finds itself closely associated with the United States of America. It is an association immediately dictated by our community of objectives, the most urgent of which is the defense of our freedom against Communist aggression. But our policy of close relations with the United States is not a mere artificial creation of government policy makers, and it is not dictated exclusively by the accident of common purposes. It is the product of experience in serving the national interest. . . .

Our freedom is the fruit of the efforts, the sacrifices, and the blood of our people. We won it by rising against Spain, by persuading America, and by resisting the Japanese. That is why our people love our freedom so much. I disagree with those who declare that we were "given" our freedom, as if it were a gift and not a right.

But if our freedom is our own, it would be hard to deny that the character of our people and our republic bears the indelible marks of our past association with other peoples. Our basic Malay traits have absorbed many of the qualities of the Chinese of the Ming invasion and of the quiet beauty of the cultures swept to our shores by the tides of several Southeast Asian empires. The culture of our people received its most permanent and most universal mark when Spain brought us the Catholic faith. And the architects of our independence so fashioned our political institutions that they are almost identical to those of the United States. . . .

The American regime was not by any means a "perfect" government. There is no substitute for complete self-government. Furthermore, although political autonomy was extended to a degree unprecedented in colonial annals, although health and education were improved to an extent which might not have been within reach of a weak independent nation, no serious effort was made to lift the population up from its ancient agricultural economy. But the hand of America was relatively light. And so invigorating were the basic freedoms she guaranteed to the individual Filipino that when the Japanese invaders landed on our shores, the Filipinos, even though complete independence had not come, resisted as if their actual sovereign, the American people, were merely their allies in the struggle for their freedom. While in some countries of Asia the Japanese were being received either indifferently or as liberators, the Filipinos resisted as though complete national liberty was theirs. . . .

I have said that our differences in outlook with some of our neighbors in Asia could be due to the different circumstances that have surrounded our histories and experiences. I want to reiterate that we are aware of these historical and other differences and respect our neighbors' rights to their own approach to international questions, even if we disagree with them. We ask only that our own position be viewed with the same understanding. . . .

If there are those who still suspect American motives, it is perhaps because, influenced by their own history, they cannot bring themselves to credit any western country with good intentions. Perhaps an increase in information about Philippine-American experience would help them to change this attitude. . . . Recently several incidents . . . have dramatized the need for the removal of certain points of friction occasioned by the existence of such (military) bases on our soil. The Communist press abroad naturally overplayed the incidents. We have been concerned about them, but we are not unduly alarmed. . . . The United States, with its readiness to discuss corrective measures and to enter into formal negotiations for the improvement of our bases agreement, with mutual regard for national dignity, has demonstrated its own desire to make out of our relations a pattern for East-West cooperation in the cause of freedom.

Indeed, that should be our joint course—in all humility to admit the possibility of imperfection and with all good will to strive for perfection. Perfection may never be reached. But in striving for it we may yet fashion a model which will attract all free men to that unity without which godliness and liberty could never be fully secure. . . .

— Reading No. 26 —

SENATOR CLARO M. RECTO: U. S.-PHILIPPINE RELATIONS, APRIL 17, 1951[1]

In the Philippines, Senator Recto has been identified with a policy of more independence and less subservience in Philippine relations with the United States. He expressed his views in a commencement address at the University of the Philippines. "In the grand English tradition, the language is elevated, the phrasing perfect and the peroration like the closing of the doors of a great cathedral."

✓   ✓   ✓

(Ten years ago) thousands of university and college cadets were marshalled by their instructors in an impressive military demonstration of loyalty to the sovereignty of the United States of America. No one then could foretell the tragic end of the parade . . . Ten years have passed since then. . . . Unhappily, the times have not changed, and small nations must still pay the price of quarrels between great powers. Already we see before our eyes a re-enactment of the tragedies of the last conflict, when in Europe and in Asia, the small nations that became the battlegrounds of the great were compelled to endure the identical horrors of conquest and liberation. . . .

Four times the capital of Seoul has suffered the process of competitive liberation. For those of us who experienced

[1] From Teodoro M. Locsin, "The Great Debate," *Philippines Free Press*, Manila, April 28, 1951, p. 2.

the liberation of Manila in 1945, where more lives were lost and more destruction resulted from the action of the liberation armies than at the hands of the maddened and desperate enemy, it is not difficult to believe that when Seoul was liberated for the fourth time last month, only one-fifth of the original population of one million and a half remained, and they were only the old, the sick, and the children. . . .

Shall we become another Korea? What have we done with our independence to make sure that our country will not again become the battleground of foreign wars? What have we done with our independence to make sure that our people will not again be deserted in the interest of higher strategy and military necessity, and left to fondle the hard comfort of another "I shall return."

The tragedy of our foreign policy is that, being an Asian people ten thousand miles away from the effective center of American power, our behavior has been that of a banana republic in the Caribbean. We have fed upon the fancy that we are somehow the favorite children of America, and that she, driven by some strange predilection for our people, will never forsake us nor sacrifice our interests to her own or to those of others for her own sake.

Yet, though we may feel the deepest admiration and respect for the American people, . . . I think it is wrong for us to believe and to act as if we believed, that American policy can ever have any objective other than the security, welfare, and interest of the American people. . . .

Yet our foreign policy was conducted from the very beginning, and is being pursued, on the erroneous assumption of an identity of American and Filipino interests, or more correctly, of the desirability, and even the necessity, of subordinating our interests to those of America . . . We followed America out of Spain and back again; we followed America in her aimless pilgrimage in the Holy Land, from Jew to Arab and Arab to Jew, as the American need for Arab oil and the American administration's desire for Jewish votes dictated; we recognized the independence of Indonesia when America did, and not one moment before. In the world parliament of the United Nations, it is no more difficult to predict that the Philippines will vote with the American Union, than that the Ukraine will vote with the Soviet Union. American policy has found no more eloquent spokesman and zealous advocate, and Russian policy no louder critic and more resourceful opponent, than the Philippines. America may disagree violently with their own foreign policy, but it has no better supporters than the Filipinos. . . .

What are the Philippines to do? It depends on what America will do.

If America really believes that war is inevitable, then let her give us in Asia a resolute leadership we can trust; let her give the same unconditional pledges and guarantees and the same actual evidence of a spirit of equality and common fate that she has given her kinsmen and allies in the Atlantic community; and we shall have the justification for the risk of war and incentive to make common cause.

Otherwise we must restrain our enthusiasms, dissemble our sympathies, moderate our words and actions, and in fulfillment of the primitive duty of self-preservation, make no enemies where we can make no friends, and hold our peace. It may be a precarious peace, of uncertain duration, at the mercy of military time tables and power politics, but if it is broken, at least, it shall not be said that we sought it, and if we are attacked, that we deserved it. . . .

Let not Macaulay's traveller from New Zealand, exploring the spectral ruins of Manila in the course of his post-atomic war peregrinations, and cautiously testing the radioactive waters of the Pasig, from the broken arches of the Quezon bridge, have cause to ponder that in those shattered tenements and poisoned fields and rivers once lived a nation unique in the annals of mankind; free men who put their liberties on the auction block, a sacrificial race who with a mysterious urge to suicide, who being weak and weaponless, took upon themselves the quarrels of the strong, and having been warned of their abandonment still persisted in their lonely course, and whose brutalized and monstrously deformed survivors, scrambling with stunted limbs in the infected debris of their liberated cities, had forgotten even the echo of the memory of the strange illusion for which their race had fought and perished.

— Reading No. 27 —

PRIME MINISTER U NU OF BURMA SPEAKS ABOUT ASIAN-U. S. RELATIONS, JULY 6, 1955[1]

In a disarmingly candid talk to the Overseas Press Club in New York, the distinguished state visitor told his audience why Asians liked and respected Americans, and why in spite of the historical reservoir of good will, some Asians looked upon some contemporary American policies with misgiving tinged with mistrust.

What do Asians think of Americans? . . .

As is only to be expected, Asians hold all sorts of views about Americans. These range all the way from those who think the Americans are heroes, brave men and women, whose mission is to make the world happier for all, to those who see Americans as a race of warmongers, spoiling for a fight, and ready to doom the world to an atomic holocaust.

Those who think of the Americans as heroes do so because of your history, your experience, your traditions, and your devotion to the principles of freedom and democracy. America was the source of those ideas and moral principles of government that have been the inspiration and hope of Asia for more than half a century. Among them are the following:

(1) All men are created equal and must be equal before the law.

(2) All men are endowed with certain inalienable

[1] *An Asian Speaks, op. cit.,* p. 21.

rights which it is wrong and immoral of any government to deny or curtail.

(3) A right and moral government is a government of the people, by the people, for the people, devoted to the greatest good of the greatest number.

(4) A right and moral government is a government of laws, not of men, which derives its just powers from the consent of the governed.

These are tremendous ideas. They are more explosive, more powerful in their effects upon world history than all the weapons in all the arsenals. As is only to be expected, they had a tremendous impact on an Asia in which there was no recognition of the equality of men; where there was little recognition of the fundamental rights of man; where governments were imposed from above, and had as their primary objective the exploitation of the people. In fact, I think it is true to say that these ideas played a leading part in inspiring Asia's fight for freedom from colonial bondage.

Nor is this the only reason why Asians think well of Americans. Your glorious record in the two world wars in which you undoubtedly saved the world from tyranny, at great sacrifice and expense, cannot be ignored or belittled even by your most severe critics; and finally your post-World War II record, in which you have given so much of your substance to help the war-devastated countries to recover and to rebuild their shattered economies is entirely without precedent in the annals of history.

With such an impressive record behind you, it is not a matter of surprise that you should have so many admirers in Asia. Indeed the surprising thing is that there should be anyone in Asia who is dubious about America and Americans. But unfortunately there are such people, and I would like now to go into the reasons for their attitude.

One very important reason for this attitude is the equivocal position which you seem to have taken in recent years on colonial issues. To an Asia which had come to regard America as the symbol of freedom, the spearhead of the attack against colonialism, and the champion of the underdog, this has indeed been not only a disappointment, but even a great shock. Some Asians have begun to wonder whether you had abandoned your heritage and your tradition. Explanations which have been given, to the effect that colonialism is dying, and that a new and even greater danger has emerged, have left nearly all of Asia unconvinced. . . . When, therefore, Asians see America compromising on this fundamental question they can hardly be blamed if they begin to think that the American philosophy may have undergone a change, and to wonder whether freedom has the same meaning in America today as it had for your founding fathers.

A second reason is similar to the first. It is an apparent change in America's attitude towards the concept of democracy and the democratic way of life. Not only has America been regarded in the past as the champion of freedom; she was also regarded as the champion of democracy throughout the world. It is therefore something of a surprise to those who put their faith in democracy and the democratic way of life when they see this great country allying itself with, and giving support to, regimes which by no stretch of the imagination can be regarded as "governments of the people, for the people, by the people. . . ."

A third source of misunderstanding between America and Asia stems from the activities and statements of some of your leaders, and a portion of your press. These are the people who are responsible for building the impressions abroad that America is a land of warmongers, thirsting for aonther war regardless of its consequences. . . . Just as some Americans talk with some justifiable pride about the tallest and biggest buildings in the world, others talk about having the biggest and latest hydrogen bombs, the fastest and largest jet bombers; and they often round off the story by giving a vivid account of what these new weapons might be capable of doing in the way of destruction on some named target in a foreign country. This has created the most unfortunate impressions in the minds of some Asians.

I personally do not believe that Americans are warmongers. You have far too much to lose to want to risk a war. I wish I could say that all Asians, or even all Burmans, feel as I do. Unfortunately, I cannot.

We all know what lies behind these apparent deviations

from the American tradition. It is your preoccupation
with communism. But this is something that we in Asia
just do not understand. The United States today is the
most powerful country in the world. It also has one
of the highest standards of living. It has earned the
esteem and the gratitude of the people of the world for
having twice in one generation saved them from fascist
tyranny. Over the years, it has earned the esteem and the
good will of all people who value freedom and the democratic way of life. These are all solid assets. In fact, I
would say that no nation in the history of the world has
occupied the predominant position which the United
States occupies today.

That is why I am constantly surprised that the United
States tends to exaggerate its fear of the menace of communism. And when a nation becomes assessed with fear,
it is no longer quite itself. It tends to resort to expediency
at the expense of principle. It tends to forget the things
which help to make it great, and begins to look for some
new means of preserving its greatness.

I am convinced that what is required to remove such
misunderstanding as exists in Asia of the United States
is for the United States to become itself, to live up to its
heritage, and to the great principles which is spawned.
If this is done, you will, I feel sure, not only remove
all such misunderstanding, but you will be surprised at
the results not only in Asia but throughout the world. . . .

SELECTED BIBLIOGRAPHY

Ball, W. M. *Nationalism and Communism in East Asia.* 2nd ed. New York: Cambridge Univ. Press, 1956.

Cady, John F. *Roots of French Imperialism in Eastern Asia.* Ithaca, New York: Cornell Univ. Press, 1954.

Chicago University (subcontractor). *The Philippines.* "Human Resources Area Files." Monograph No. 16. 4 vols. New Haven, Conn.: 1956.

Coedes, G. *Les États Hindouises d'Indochine et Indonesia. Paris:* 1948.

de Young, John E. *Village Life in Modern Thailand.* Berkeley, Cal.: University of California Press, 1955.

Dobby, E. H. G. *Southeast Asia.* 3rd ed. London: University of London, 1954.

Du Bois, Cora. *Social Forces in Southeast Asia.* Minneapolis: University of Minnesota Press, 1949.

Elsbree, Willard H. *Japan's Role in Southeast Asian Nationalist Movements, 1940-1945.* Cambridge: Harvard Univ. Press, 1953.

Emerson, Rupert. *Representative Government in Southeast Asia.* Cambridge: Harvard Univ. Press, 1955.

Fall, Bernard B. *The Viet Minh Regime.* Rev. ed. New York: Institute of Pacific Relations, 1956.

Furnivall, J. S. *Colonial Policy and Practice.* New York: New York University Press, 1956.

Hall, D. G. E. *History of Southeast Asia.* New York: St. Martin's Press, 1955.

Hammer, Ellen J. *Struggle for Indochina.* Stanford, Cal.: Stanford University Press, 1954.

Harrison, Brian. *Southeast Asia, A Short History.* New York: St. Martin's Press, 1954.

Henniker, M. C. A. *Red Shadow over Malaya.* London: William Blackwood and Sons, 1955.

Jones, F. C. *Japan's New Order in East Asia, Its Rise and Fall.* New York: Oxford Press, 1954.

184 SELECTED BIBLIOGRAPHY

Kahin, George McT. *Nationalism and Revolution in Indonesia.* Ithaca, New York: Cornell Univ. Press, 1955.

King, Frank H. H. *New Malayan Nation.* New York: Institute of Pacific Relations, 1957.

King, John Kerry. *Southeast Asia in Perspective.* New York: The Macmillan Co., 1956.

Landon, Kenneth P. *Southeast Asia, Crossroad of Religions.* Chicago: University of Chicago Press, 1949.

Le May, Reginald. *The Culture of Southeast Asia.* London: George Allen and Unwin, 1954.

Purcell, Victor. *Chinese in Southeast Asia.* New York: Oxford Press, 1951.

————. *Colonial Period in Southeast Asia.* New York: Institute of Pacific Relations, 1953.

Royal Institute of International Affairs. *Collective Defence in Southeast Asia.* New York: Oxford Press, 1956.

Skinner, G. William. *Chinese Society in Thailand.* Ithaca, New York: Cornell Univ. Press, 1957.

Spencer, Joseph. *Asia, East by South.* New York: Wiley & Sons, 1954.

Thompson, Virginia, and Adloff, Richard. *Minority Problems in Southeast Asia.* Stanford, Cal.: Stanford Univ. Press, 1955.

Tinker, Hugh. *Union of Burma.* London: Oxford Press, 1957.

Wertheim, W. F. *Indonesian Society in Transition.* The Hague and Bandung: W. Van Hoeve, 1956.

Winstedt, Sir Richard O. *Malaya and its History.* 4th ed. London: Hutchinson's University Library, 1956.

Wurzburg, C. E. *Raffles of the Eastern Isles.* London: Hodder and Stoughton, 1954.

Zinkin, Maurice. *Development for Free Asia.* Fairlawn, New Jersey: Essential Books, Inc., 1956.

INDEX

185

VAN NOSTRAND ANVIL BOOKS already published